PURPLE
Reign

HOW GRAND ISLAND BECAME A NEBRASKA WRESTLING DYNASTY

BY MIKE SCHADWINKEL
WITH CRAIG SESKER

PURPLE REIGN
How Grand Island became
a Nebraska wrestling dynasty

By Mike Schadwinkel
With Craig Sesker

Copyright: 2019 Mike Schadwinkel and Craig Sesker
Sponsorship: Trey Mytty
Edited by Anne Sesker
Designed by Angie Hardenbrook
Cover design by Ben Strandberg
Photos by *Omaha World-Herald,* Jen Leetch
Published by Kingery Printing
Cost: $20.00

No part of this book may be reproduced or transmitted in any form or by any means, electronic or mechanical, including photocopying, recording, or by any information storage and retrieval system, without permission in writing from the publisher.

Printed in the United States of America

First Edition

FOREWORD

By Joe Kutlas
Former athletic director, Grand Island Senior High

Winning a state championship is a difficult thing to do in any sport – most high school athletes and coaches toil, sweat, train, dream. And never have the experience. To win five *straight* Class A wrestling titles and then a state dual tournament title after that? Set the Class A scoring record? Have an impressive march of individual state champs and dozens of medal winners in the run? It takes a perfect storm of talent, focused and determined effort, the creation of a culture of excellence, tremendous technical and motivational coaching, an unwavering work ethic in the off-season, and the support of a lot of folks from boosters, to parents, to youth programs, to the school. We had all of that at Grand Island Senior High over a glorious title run from 2009-2014.

And we had the architect and engineer: Mike Schadwinkel.

This is the story of those state title years at Grand Island Senior High and the story of Coach Schadwinkel. Where he started, the path he took, and where he stands today. It's about his plan for Grand Island wrestling, and the execution of that plan. And about the people who contributed mightily along the way. Coach Schad will lay out, in detail, the many triumphs of the Islanders' unbelievable state title run – the sacrifices, the work and the sweat, the setbacks, the sweet victories, the relationships and the pivotal

PURPLE REIGN

moments. He'll give well-deserved mention and credit to many, many of the athletes and coaches he worked with.

I've enjoyed reading the draft of Mike's book – recalling the specific memories and the big matches and so many wrestlers I pulled for and ached for as the athletic director. There were so many times of unbridled exhilaration. But a few thoughts and people stand out for me to mention before you dive into what Mike has to say.

Andrew Riedy. And, yes, winning four state individual titles would be enough. But it was the way he did it. He was a great athlete, for sure, but that was only the start. What put him over the top was the work ethic, on the mat and in the classroom. He excelled in both arenas because excellence was a habit for him. His technical ability, as Mike will detail, was superior, as were his mat smarts. Never showy, he let his work on the mat do the talking. A gritty leader by example, Andrew rose up in the biggest moments. And much of the credit goes to Andrew's father, Coach Rob Riedy, who was one of my favorite folks to work with during this great GISH wrestling run. Coach Riedy was tremendous with *all* of our athletes. He was a visionary who beautifully complemented the other strengths on our wrestling staff, and he *knew* wrestling.

Andrew was the foundation in the room during that championship run. But others captured my mind and heart: from Chase Reis, to Daniel Sotelo, Billy Thompson, Carlos Rodriguez, Nate Westerby and Riley Allen. And many others, of course. Young men with determination, and often interesting backstories – young men you couldn't help but cheer for. They deserved the support by virtue of what they'd done, or overcome, or just because of who they were as people and competitors. The depth of will, desire, and talent in our wrestling room was simply amazing. I appreciate all of those wrestlers who left it all up there each day.

Al Hayman. Never was a "custodian" more important to a wrestling program. Al was actually more of an Assistant Athletic Director in Charge of Wrestling Operations. Al didn't just love wrestling – he had the work ethic and the knowledge and the pride to do absolutely whatever it took to host a first-class wrestling event. Whatever needed to be done, Al did it. He not only never complained about the additional workload or long hours, instead he asked, "What else can we do? What else can I do?" He was like that about everything at GISH, but particularly about his passion: wrestling. Greg Uhrmacher, Chris Ladwig, Maria Tomlin and Renee Albers, my long-time activities office staff, also never flinched when it came to support of GISH athletics and Islander wrestling. And the same could emphatically be said of our administrative team, who steadfastly, through good times and bad, supported our teams, coaches, and athletes, and kept a steady eye on all the prizes that mattered.

The Flatwater Fracas. This was Schad's dream. He kept hammering at me, the old basketball coach, until I saw the light. With most of the top teams in Class A and B in Nebraska participating, and a nice out-of-state flavor, the 32-team, two-day dual tournament eventually became the biggest wrestling event in Nebraska, outside of the state tournaments. It took a lot of people, and great effort and support from the school and community to get it there. We were all exhausted when it was over, but also extremely proud. The event also provided one of the sweetest wrestling memories for me: the victory over Billings Skyview. Those of us at the scorers' table were busy crunching numbers when we got down 33-11 – trying to figure out if we still had a mathematical chance to win the dual even with a few pins mixed in. And then it happened. Match-by-match, the miracle happened. That was an afternoon to remember.

Our schedule. Schad always wanted the tough schedule: the rougher the better. He was never looking to pad the win total; instead, he was always looking to toughen up his wrestlers, to expose their weaknesses so they could work on them. He wanted them to face the best competition he could provide, even if that meant traveling a great distance. Mike didn't just agree to wrestle anyone at any time, he sought out those opportunities. And it paid off. His wrestlers were battled-tested and confident. They became better skilled by facing a constant fire. There was an aura about them. I truly believe other schools and other wrestlers were intimidated by them. They knew what our guys had done and it worried them.

The first state title. Dethroning and dominating a powerhouse program like Millard South and setting a Class A scoring record was impressive. The title was in-hand after Friday night, so Saturday was... just so great. And so great not just because the Class A title was wrapped up, but because the hits just kept coming. The Islander wrestlers came up big, match after match, and put an exclamation point on the tournament and the changing of the guard in Class A. It was a special, special weekend.

Adversity. You're always walking that fine line with some athletes. You want them to be tough, to be a little ornery, to be unafraid. That sometimes means kids will use bad judgement. They will cross the line, and our Islander wrestlers sometimes did. I know that some viewed our crew as outlaws, in the worst of moments. But they never saw what was happening behind the scenes. I saw it. I saw Mike's daily efforts, his view of the big picture, his anguish when kids made mistakes, and his consistent desire to educate kids, to help mold kids into better people. While Mike worked hard to create and foster an unshakable confidence in his athletes, he also expected them to respect the team, the sport, the school and themselves. And he held them accountable, disciplined them and worked with them when they didn't meet the character bar. He wanted to win, and win big, as we all did, athletes and parents included. But it was never without a view to the long haul, the life and the character Mike wanted to develop in his athletes.

Finally, let me say this: I so enjoyed Mike Schadwinkel, the collegiate Academic All-American. The smiling, caring, intelligent guy I worked closely with and enjoyed as a colleague and friend. I loved watching him work with kids, and loved watching him celebrate team and individual successes. But some of my favorite memories with Mike were simply sitting in my office and talking. He's a sharp guy with many interests. He knew what was going on in the world, outside of his sport, and was simply fun to visit with. He is entertaining and aware – a solid, committed husband and father. I felt, and still feel, very lucky to have been associated with Mike.

HOW GRAND ISLAND BECAME A NEBRASKA WRESTLING DYNASTY

Watching him coach… was, well, the man can coach. He can motivate, he can teach, he can plan, and he can get kids to reach down and give their best.

It was quite a ride. Enjoy the book...

CHAPTER 1
RUNNING DOWN A DREAM

I have fond memories of my childhood days. I love where I grew up. I spent my early years in my hometown of Alliance. I grew up in the scenic High Plains of Nebraska in a relatively remote area of the country without many neighboring communities.

Alliance is located closer to the Colorado, Wyoming and South Dakota borders than it is to the largest Nebraska cities of Omaha and Lincoln.

There were plenty of wide-open spaces where I grew up on the far western edge of the Nebraska sandhills. It is an area with a fairly high elevation of nearly 4,000 feet.

Hemingford, situated 20 miles to the northwest, is the closest town to Alliance. The next-closest is Bridgeport, located 36 miles to the south.

The Nebraska state capital of Lincoln is a seven-hour drive from Alliance. Omaha, the state's largest city, is almost eight hours away.

Where I grew up, people are recognized for their strong work ethics. They make their living as railroaders, ranchers and farmers.

And they aren't afraid of putting in long days to get their jobs done.

My father, Charles "Chick" Schadwinkel, was one of those hard workers.

My dad was an engineer for Burlington Santa Fe Railroad. He pulled coal trains following Nebraska Highway 2 through the sand-

PURPLE REIGN

hills to Ravenna, Nebraska, and then brought back the empty ones.

My dad was making two or three runs a week on the railroad and would be gone for a couple of days and then back home for a couple of days before he left again.

He was a very disciplined, regimented man who definitely did things the right way. He was tough on me and my brothers – he taught us to be disciplined, responsible and hard-working.

He led the way for us.

As he got older, my father was very supportive of what I did in athletics. He was arguably my biggest fan when I competed and when I coached.

He was always there when he could be. He was very proud of anything I accomplished, and that meant a lot to me.

My mother, Mary, was an English teacher. She was very active at Alliance High School. She was the cheerleading sponsor, and she was involved with the student council. She was very well-liked in the school and the community.

She is an awesome mom who has always been very devoted to our family.

I am the oldest of three boys. My brother, Andy, was born 20 months after I was. He was one grade behind me in school. David is the baby, and he is almost eight years younger than me.

Andy and David dabbled in wrestling while growing up. Andy ended up playing basketball in high school, and David wrestled a couple of years in high school.

Andy and I were the best of friends and the worst of enemies. He was my best competitor. We were always throwing the football and baseball.

We were very competitive – we didn't like to lose, especially to each other.

I've always felt we were a part of a very fortunate time in Alliance. There were a number of good athletes at our school. We were teammates on a football team that went undefeated and made the state playoffs.

Andy is very smart. He definitely surpassed me with his achievements in the classroom. He had straight A's all the way

HOW GRAND ISLAND BECAME A NEBRASKA WRESTLING DYNASTY

through high school. I had good grades, but he really excelled.

Because David is so much younger, we weren't as close growing up. He was still in elementary school when I graduated from high school. He played tennis and golfed in college for Nebraska Wesleyan. He went on and joined the U.S. Air Force.

My brothers are dynamic, great people who have gone on to be very successful. I'm very proud of them.

Alliance, with a population just under 10,000 people, was the ideal place for an aspiring young wrestler like me to grow up in during the 1980s.

Alliance High School was a powerhouse in wrestling, winning four state championships among seven top-three state finishes from 1972-87.

They won their first state team title in Class B in 1972 with 126-pound champion Dennis Girard leading the way.

Just over a decade later, Alliance engineered a three-peat. The Bulldogs claimed the Class B state team title in 1985 before moving up to the state's biggest class and winning Class A state championships in 1986 and 1987.

Alliance achieved an incredible feat by setting the Class B state scoring record in 1985 before setting the Class A scoring record a year later in 1986.

They went toe-to-toe with the state's biggest schools from Omaha and Lincoln in Class A. And they beat them all.

Ironically, the power in high school wrestling then largely resided in the panhandle.

In 1986, three of the four state champions were from that part of the state. In addition to Alliance winning that year in Class A, Gering won state in Class B and Rushville won state in Class D.

Looking back, it was really amazing and impressive what Alliance accomplished.

Those were some unbelievable teams – those guys were as fearless as they were tough. They were rough, mean and competitive. And they had great coaching with Pat Cullen and Duane Dobson.

Cullen was a great motivator and was tough on kids, but he

PURPLE REIGN

also showed great compassion. Those are the characteristics of a successful coach.

Dobson was the technician, demonstrating moves and techniques to use in a match. He also held people accountable. Both men had a big impact on me as a wrestler and a ton of influence on my coaching.

I was very fortunate to learn from Coach Cullen and Coach Dobson.

They had quite the stable of studs.

Randy Hansen, Bill Alvarado and Scott Rand won Class B state titles for Alliance in 1985. Rand and Kory Piihl won Class A state crowns in 1986 with Piihl, Mike Schnell and Jeff Colwell striking Class A state gold in 1987.

I loved watching those guys wrestle. They were some tough, tough dudes.

I had a front row seat for all of it. I went to the home matches at Alliance High School, and I watched them compete.

They inspired me and motivated me. I watched what they did, and they showed me what was possible. Watching those teams was the beginning of formulating my dreams of being a state champion.

I knew all about the Alliance tradition from an early age. My father was a member of the first Bulldogs wrestling team in 1961. Alliance's Chuck Krantz was Nebraska's state chairman with USA Wrestling for quite a bit of my youth.

We were in a great situation with all the resources we had available. Alliance was a hub in wrestling – especially for freestyle wrestling.

My introduction to the sport of wrestling came when I was five years old.

When I was in first grade, I wrote about the sport for one of my classes at school:

"I am a wrestler. I love wrestling. It's my favorite sport. I pin some kids. I have lots and lots of fun."

I started tagging along to practices at a very young age with Scott Dobson, son of Alliance assistant coach Duane Dobson.

Duane Dobson wrestled for the University of Nebraska, and

he was obviously very knowledgeable about the sport. He had plenty to offer for a young kid who was new to wrestling.

I was eager to learn, and he had a lot to teach me.

Scott and I were part of a group of neighborhood kids that grew up and played all the sports together.

Whatever sport was in season was my favorite.

I started playing four sports in high school – football, wrestling, track and baseball.

My mom thought that my best sport wasn't any of the ones that I played in high school.

She thought my best sport was swimming.

As a kid, we had a swim team in my hometown. We had a city pool, and we would go swim in the mornings and train a little bit.

There were a group of towns in Nebraska, Wyoming and Colorado that had swim teams. Each town would host a swim meet throughout the summer.

I had a lot of success and a lot of fun. I held many records in that little swim group.

My favorite events were butterfly and breaststroke, but I would kill it in freestyle.

The one event I always hated was the backstroke.

My favorite event was the individual medley. It was one lap of the pool in each of the four strokes.

I competed in swimming from the time I was around 7 years old until I was 12. We didn't have a swim team at our high school.

My mom still thinks if there had been a strong swimming program that I might have participated in high school.

I liked swimming. It was a really cool experience for a kid, winning a lot of medals and ribbons while traveling around to different places to compete. It was a blast.

I probably had more success in swimming in those days than I did in wrestling. But for some reason, I just kept wanting to wrestle.

Growing up, I had so much fun playing as many sports as I could.

I eventually narrowed down the list of sports I played to foot-

PURPLE REIGN

ball and wrestling.

I had my most success in wrestling.

I began in kindergarten. We had practices, and learned basic moves and fundamentals. Then we wrestled in a small community wrestling meet against kids from our town.

I definitely liked to wrestle, but at that time it was just one of the sports I was playing along with basketball, soccer, baseball and swimming. At that age, we wrestled freestyle from March through early May and then played baseball in the summer. We played whatever sport was in season.

My love of sports was evident in a paper I still have from fourth grade:

"I want to wrestle in the Olympics. I want to swim in the Olympics. I want to be able to do millions of things. I want to be a fullback and a kicker for the Nebraska Cornhuskers. I'm going to be on TV in every sport there is. I want to wrestle, play soccer, football, swim, play tennis, basketball, do gymnastics, volleyball and boxing. I'm going to be the highest ranked player there is in every sport."

Youth sports seasons were shorter then, and kids had the opportunity to play a lot of different sports, which was fun for me.

There wasn't as much specialization as there is now in so many sports.

I was playing virtually every sport that I could.

And I loved it.

When I was in first grade, I won my first wrestling tournament. And then I didn't win another tournament for a couple of years.

It was very tough in the beginning. I didn't win tournaments consistently until middle school and then everything started to come together for me.

I only lost two matches in my seventh- and eighth-grade folkstyle seasons while wrestling for Alliance Middle School.

Early in my wrestling career, I remember watching the 1984 Olympic Games on television and that caught my attention.

That's the first time that I became excited about wrestling and thinking maybe I wanted to do this at a high level.

What I remember most was watching Bruce Baumgartner compete when the Olympics were held in Los Angeles in 1984. Bruce won the Olympic gold medal for the United States at heavyweight. He really stood out to me. He was a big, strong, powerful guy who was really impressive. He wrestled like a lot of the smaller guys because he could scramble and move around really well.

And it was fun watching Dave and Mark Schultz win gold medals. And then seeing Bobby Weaver running around and celebrating after he won was really awesome.

The U.S. won seven gold medals in freestyle wrestling at the 1984 Olympics in L.A.

Seeing the athletes stand on top of the podium with our national anthem playing and our flag being raised had a big impact on me.

I was 10 years old and watching the Olympics showed me what someone could achieve in wrestling. It was really exciting to see what the possibilities were.

At that point, I decided that I wanted to be an Olympic gold medalist.

I had my share of success on the mat, but I also battled my share of adversity during my high school wrestling career.

I was a four-sport athlete during my first two years of high school before narrowing my focus to football and wrestling.

I landed a spot in the varsity lineup as a freshman at Alliance High School. But being a freshman at a heavier weight class of 171 pounds was extremely tough. Most of the opponents I wrestled were upperclassmen who were more mature and physically developed than I was.

I took my share of lumps that year. I had a 10-20 record – it was a rough season and it was frustrating. But I still almost made it to state.

I made it to the blood round at districts, the pressure-packed round where the winner goes to state and the loser is done for the season. I was battling an upperclassman from Kearney and was winning late in the match. My dream of qualifying for state as a

PURPLE REIGN

freshman was within reach. But I lost on a reversal at the end of the match and ended my season one win away from state.

It was pretty heartbreaking. And motivating.

My sophomore year, I was much-improved. I was 24-8 going into the district tournament and was seeded third at 189 pounds. I was upset in the first round and had to come back through the backside of the bracket. We were wrestling in the old gym in Grand Island, where I later taught physical education and coached for a number of years.

The No. 1 seed had been upset, so I had to wrestle him in the match to go to state. I lost the match, and I vividly remember bawling my eyes out.

It was a crushing defeat. I couldn't believe I wasn't going to state. I was devastated.

I was definitely starting to have some success in wrestling at the high-school level, but it wasn't anywhere close to what I wanted.

I made a decision that day that would fuel and drive me for the next two years. I was going to win a state championship.

I started working out and training a lot more. I dedicated myself more to wrestling. And then I gave up track and baseball my last two years of high school.

I remember thinking I was wasting time in those sports when I could do a harder workout in a much shorter period that would help me in wrestling and football.

I learned another hard lesson right before my junior year at Alliance High.

Toward the end of that summer, I got in trouble. I was out with some friends and we got caught with alcohol. We were out on a country road with beer and the cops nailed us. It was still summer, but just a few weeks before football season.

A police officer called my parents and told them. My mom and dad knew about it even before I made it home that night.

My parents obviously were not happy. They decided my punishment was going to be sitting out the first two football games of my junior year.

HOW GRAND ISLAND BECAME A NEBRASKA WRESTLING DYNASTY

My parents were very wise to do what they did. They took away what was most important to me. Ultimately, I learned my lesson.

My parents talked to me about what happened. They yelled some, too, about my poor decisions.

They came down on me pretty hard. They obviously were disappointed and wisely wanted me to suffer the consequences.

At that point, I made the decision to stop raising so much hell. I started focusing more on sports and school.

I came back after my suspension and earned a starting spot on the football team. We landed a berth in the state playoffs in Class A.

We played in the state's biggest class with schools from the larger metropolitan cities of Omaha and Lincoln.

We had a great turnaround in football that year. We got off to a rough start, losing our first three games, but then we really put it together. I became a starter on the defensive line. I didn't play the first two games and neither did my buddy, Mitch Kampbell, a starter on the offensive line. I'm pretty sure our parents collaborated on our punishments.

When we returned to the team, we played well. We got hot and won our last six games and made the playoffs.

The week the playoffs were about to start, the eastern part of the state was pounded with a snowstorm.

Our playoff game at Omaha Westside was moved to Memorial Stadium in Lincoln because it was artificial turf and it was easier to remove the snow. We played at the college stadium where the University of Nebraska plays. It was a pretty cool experience playing there even though we ended up losing the game 21-3.

I immediately shifted gears and began preparing for my junior season in wrestling at 189 pounds.

I was excited for an opportunity to finally make it to state.

I went 32-4 and had a great year.

I'm not sure if I was even ranked that year, but I made it to the state championship match.

I was really strong at turning guys on the mat and that's where

PURPLE REIGN

I excelled in wrestling. I would cross-face guys and turn them, and I would cradle my opponents.

I advanced to the finals against a very powerful and explosive athlete, Omaha North senior Clinton Childs.

Clinton went on to play running back for the University of Nebraska on their national championship teams in the 1990s.

The match didn't go well for me. Clinton scored a couple of early takedowns and then it snowballed in his favor. I started taking bad shots and he added a few takedowns on go-behinds. He won the match by an 18-7 major decision.

Clinton was a really physical wrestler and a very tough opponent.

Before the match, I went and warmed up for two hours. By the time I went out there for the match, I wasn't mentally or physically ready to wrestle. I shouldn't have spent that much time warming up. I'm not saying I would've won the match, but it wasn't the best approach for me to warm up for that long.

I fell short of my ultimate goal my junior season, but I was still as driven as ever to reach my goals.

I was looking forward to my senior season with high expectations in football and wrestling.

My senior year in football, we were undefeated in the regular season. We were the No. 1 seed going into the playoffs. Lincoln Southeast was the powerhouse in Class A. They were nationally ranked, but they had lost a game to Kansas City Rockhurst.

Southeast then lost to Fremont in a rainstorm at the end of the regular season and they dropped to the No. 8 seed for the playoffs.

Southeast had to come to Alliance to play against us in the first round of the playoffs. That was the worst possible draw for us. They had multiple guys who went on to play Division I football – they were loaded with outstanding players. We were outmanned.

We jumped out to a 10-7 lead by halftime, but they came back. We ended up losing the game 28-17. We played a good game, but they had a better team.

It was disappointing, but I had to move past it. I had bigger goals I wanted to accomplish.

HOW GRAND ISLAND BECAME A NEBRASKA WRESTLING DYNASTY

My final high school football season had ended, but now I was ready to pursue a state title in wrestling.

I was ranked No. 1 in the state in Class A my entire senior season at 189 pounds.

I was on a mission. From the day I lost that match to Clinton Childs in the state finals my junior year until the state tournament the next year, I told myself it was going to happen. I was going to win a state title.

There was not a shred of doubt in my mind. I trained for it all spring and all summer. I did extra running and weightlifting. And I hit every freestyle practice.

The only break I took from my training for wrestling was during football season. And we still did our share of lifting and conditioning for football.

When wrestling season started, I was ready to go.

I won districts and was the favorite going into the 1993 state tournament.

I was able to come out strong at state.

I had two pins before winning handily in the semifinals to make the state championship match for the second straight year.

I achieved one of my biggest goals when I edged Demetrius Richards of Omaha Central 5-4 in the Class A 189-pound state championship match at the Devaney Center in in 1993 in Lincoln.

Richards came out and scored the first takedown before I got a reversal and rode him out in the first period. I was up 4-2 late in the match, but he got a takedown to tie it 4-4. There was a stoppage in the match and I remember looking at the clock. There were 20 seconds left.

The pressure was on and the stakes were high, but I was calm as I walked back to the center of the mat. I knew I was going to win.

All I had to do was get out and the state title I had worked so hard for was mine.

The referee blew the whistle and I exploded to my feet. I got right up and got right out. I escaped and then held him off in the final seconds to win the match 5-4.

I raised my arms when I won the state title. I was definitely

PURPLE REIGN

excited to win because it was a culmination of two full years of hard work and all of the years I wrestled before that.

This was the ultimate at that stage of my life.

I believed it was going to happen. I remember hugging my coaches and smiling a lot after I won.

I did it. I had won state. It was a relief to win. I was a state champion.

There is definitely something special about setting a lofty goal and achieving it. That was an experience I could identify with when the wrestlers I went on to coach were trying to do the same thing.

My state title came two years after my good friend, Scott Dobson, had captured a Class A state title for Alliance at 130 pounds in 1991.

It was an awesome atmosphere to wrestle in at the Devaney Center.

It was a special moment to win a state title. It meant a lot to be able to share it with my coaches and teammates. And above all, to share it with my family.

Even though my high school football career had ended the previous fall, I had one final opportunity to play football at the prep level.

I had earned second team all-state honors in football as a lineman, and I was selected to play in the Nebraska Shrine Bowl all-star football game alongside the state's best high school players.

The game was held the summer after I graduated from Alliance High School.

I was on the same team at the Shrine Bowl as quarterback Scott Frost, who went on to lead Nebraska to a national title in 1997 before eventually becoming the Cornhusker head football coach in 2017.

There was a crazy amount of talent in that Shrine Bowl, but Frost was the star of the show. There was media around him the entire time. Frost was unbelievable. He was fast, tall and athletic. He could run the ball and he could throw it.

There ended up being eight or nine guys in that game that played on the 1997 national championship team for Nebraska. Frost was unbelievable. He was fast and tall and athletic.

I was a 6-foot-1, 210-pound lineman, but Frost was bigger than me and he was a quarterback. He was already 6-foot-3 and 215 pounds. We were on the same team, but I played defense in the game.

I was excited to see Nebraska hire Frost as their coach. He is as close to a modern-day Tom Osborne as we are going to get. I think he will do really well as the coach at Nebraska.

I wasn't recruited nearly as heavily as Frost was, but I was recruited coming out of high school by a number of schools for football and wrestling.

Nearby Chadron State offered me a scholarship for football and wrestling. NCAA Division II power Nebraska-Omaha offered me a chance to wrestle. UNO head wrestling coach Mike Denney made a great offer to me and I strongly considered it.

I really liked Coach Denney and I liked UNO, but it was a little intimidating and scary for me to go to Omaha.

I contemplated playing both sports in college. Wrestling was my best sport, but I really loved playing football.

Ultimately, I accepted a scholarship offer to wrestle for Adams State College in Alamosa, Colorado. My high school coach, Dale Hall, was a national champion for Adams State. The Indians had won an NAIA national title in wrestling just a few years before in 1990.

Hall is the older brother of Dennis Hall, a world champion and Olympic silver medalist in Greco-Roman wrestling.

Adams State was a blessing for me. God put me there because he wanted me to persevere. I fought through a lot of adversity, and I was a long way from home.

It was an experience that really shaped me into the person that I am today.

I became a four-year starter for Adams State, earning my bachelor's and master's degrees. I qualified for the NCAA Division II national tournament three times, placing fourth as a junior and second as a senior.

To say my first couple of years were a struggle at Adams State

PURPLE REIGN

would be an understatement.

The grind of a college wrestling season isn't for everybody. It's a long season and it's tough.

Nearly every guy in our wrestling room was a star in high school. They were used to winning and they were highly competitive. And confident. They didn't like losing, even during practice.

The athletes at the college level are very physical. Making weight every week during the college season takes a significant toll on you.

Adams State had a good wrestling program and it was a strong school academically.

It was a tough transition to college. I had a miserable freshman year in wrestling.

The plan was for me to redshirt, meaning I would gain experience by wrestling in open tournaments while not using a year of eligibility. Most wrestlers will redshirt during their first year in order to help them with the transition from high school to college.

We wrestled at the Cowboy Open in Wyoming at the start of the season. I was pumped up and ready to go. And I had a few butterflies in my stomach as well. It was my first college tournament.

I went out on the mat and my opponent shot in on my leg and I was defending a single-leg attack. I sprained my knee pretty badly. It was the first period of my first match and I was done for the day. I couldn't believe it.

I was out for a couple of weeks with the injury. I came back and started training again, and the coaches at Adams State were talking about pulling my redshirt. But then I ended up contracting a serious skin infection and I was sidelined again.

I then had a hernia operation over Christmas break and I was out for another month. I finished my redshirt season with a 1-3 record. I wrestled four times and lost three of them.

I'm sure my coaches were wondering why they were putting so much money into a kid who only won one match that season.

I finally was cleared to return to practice in February, and I was able to get in some good training with some good guys on our team. I ended a rough season on a positive note.

HOW GRAND ISLAND BECAME A NEBRASKA WRESTLING DYNASTY

I returned home that summer and followed a weightlifting program given to the team by our coach. I lifted religiously. And I also worked as a lifeguard at the swimming pool.

I came back for my second year at Adams State and made the starting lineup at 177 pounds as a redshirt freshman.

I had around a .500 record that season. I grew a lot in my wrestling that year. I placed fourth in the regional tournament that season. The top three finishers were automatic qualifiers for the national tournament. They gave one wild card spot for nationals, but I wasn't picked for the wild card. I came up just short. I lost a one-point match in the third-place match, so I knew I was right there.

I came back the next season as a sophomore to a lot of changes.

Coach Rodger Jehlicka had lost two graduate assistants in Tom Dodd and Rich Straub, as well as Matt Zene, an ASC All-American. We also had graduated a strong class of seniors.

I was cutting pretty hard to make 177 and we had some tough guys in the room. I was getting beat on and tortured every day in practice. There were days I left practice in tears because I was so tired of getting beat on.

One of those guys who kicked my butt was graduate assistant coach Rob Llorca, who had been a two-time NCAA Division III national champion. He and Joe Bunning, who ended up placing third in the country for us that season at 190 pounds, made for some challenging groups of three in practice. Joe was really good, and he was very tough to wrestle in the room.

When I went home for Christmas in December 1995, I was ready to give up on college wrestling.

I walked into my parents' house and I pulled my dad aside. Some of my friends at home had left college and were working on the railroad and making over $30,000 a year. They were making damn good money for someone just 20-21 years old.

I was thinking maybe that was something that I could do.

I sat my dad down and told him what I was thinking.

I looked at him and shook my head in frustration.

PURPLE REIGN

"Dad, I don't think I can do this anymore. I'm tired of wrestling. I'm getting beat on every day."

I expected my dad to say, "Yeah, we love you. Come on home and we'll help you and get you going."

But he didn't.

He scolded me and put his finger right in front of my face.

"You made a commitment to those people," my father said. "They gave you scholarship money and you're going to get your ass back down there and you're going to finish this up."

My eyes welled up with tears. I was broken and tired and beaten up.

I didn't think I could take it anymore.

My father shocked the heck out of me with the absolute most disastrous, in my mind, reaction to what I had said. It was not what I was expecting.

I grew up fearing my dad to a certain degree. He definitely wasn't the nurturer in our household. If I needed something, I would go to my mom first.

My relationship with my dad was different at that point. I was grown up and I was wrestling in college, and he loved that. He loved that I was good at sports and he had followed my career closely through high school and college.

His tough love threw me off. It was absolutely the right thing at the right time.

It was a huge turning point in my life. It's affected my life in every way since.

I went back to school and gritted my teeth and got right back in there. I shut my mouth and went back to work. I did what my dad told me to do.

I came on late in the season, won the conference tournament at 177 and finished second at the regional tournament to Portland State's Travis Bonneau, who was ranked No. 1 in the nation. Bonneau had placed third at nationals the year before.

We both lost in the first round of the 1996 national tournament in Greeley, Colorado. And the way the brackets were set up, I would face Travis in my next match in the wrestlebacks.

HOW GRAND ISLAND BECAME A NEBRASKA WRESTLING DYNASTY

The match went into overtime. He attempted to throw me on the edge of the mat, but I stopped him and ended up pinning him.

It was a huge win for me. I had knocked off the No. 1 guy in the nation, but I lost the next match.

I was one match away from placing and didn't make it. It was disappointing. I was upset and heartbroken. I wanted to be an All-American at the NCAA Division II level.

I went back to Adams State for my junior season and I was on a mission again. I trained really hard that summer and I was ready to go.

I was cutting pretty hard to make 177 again after coming into the school year around 215 pounds.

During the middle of the season, Coach Jehlicka came to me and two of my teammates with a recommendation.

He wanted each of us to bump up a weight class.

It was after Christmas, but that news felt like Christmas morning to me.

The first thing I did after being told I was moving up a weight class was go out to eat with my girlfriend.

I had gone in to cut weight that night and came out wanting to take her out to eat. She must have thought I was crazy, but I had just learned I was moving up a weight class.

In January of my junior season, I was moving up to 190 pounds. I loved it. I could eat more, and I felt stronger and healthier. I could worry more about training and less about weight cutting. I was a little undersized at 190, but after wrestling 177 the guys at 190 felt slow. The move to a bigger weight class felt great to me. I thought I could dance circles around those heavier guys because they were so slow. My energy level was so much higher. The timing couldn't have been better for me to move up a weight class.

There was a guy from Cozad who wrestled at Chadron State named Corey Arndt. He was tall, long and rangy – he was a difficult matchup for me. He was a thorn in my side. I couldn't beat the guy.

He beat me in both of my homecoming events in Chadron when I returned to wrestle near where I grew up in Nebraska. He

PURPLE REIGN

beat me in a dual at Chadron State and again at the regional tournament there.

Corey beat me in the regional semifinals, but I was able to come back and finish third at the NCAA Division II West Regional.

I made it back to nationals. We went up to Fargo, North Dakota to compete for the NCAA Division II Championships in March of 1997. There was so much snow on the ground up that we were driving through tunnels to get to the arena. The snow was over our heads. It was miserable.

The winters in North Dakota make the winters in Nebraska seem mild.

I started off with a setback in my first match at nationals.

I lost my first-round match to a guy from Southern Illinois Edwardsville. I went on bottom and this guy put the legs in and tortured me. I ended up losing the match soundly, by 8 or 9 points. I was devastated. I went up there to be an All-American and now I found myself on the backside of the bracket.

It's a huge uphill battle when you lose first round at a big tournament like nationals.

But I was determined. And I fought back.

Ryan Wolters of North Dakota State, a national champion two years before, had lost in the quarterfinals. And now I needed to beat him to land a spot on the medal podium.

I initially allowed negative thoughts to creep into my mind. I felt like I was going to lose and not become the All-American I had so desired.

But somehow, I flipped the switch for that match. I decided I came there to be an All-American.

Before the match, I kept repeating the same thing to myself. "I'm gonna win, I'm gonna win, I'm gonna win." I bet I said it at least a thousand times. I kept saying that to myself for the next half an hour before I wrestled him. I had never done anything like that before.

I went out there to wrestle and I took Wolters down right away and rode him. This was in his home gym at North Dakota State. He was a two-time All-American and a national champion, but during

HOW GRAND ISLAND BECAME A NEBRASKA WRESTLING DYNASTY

the match there was never a moment of doubt in my mind.

In the second period, he reversed me. But I escaped and took him back down. Then I turned him and pinned him. I shook his hand, walked off the mat and I was so happy to be an All-American. It's something I really, really wanted and I felt good about accomplishing it.

I had landed a spot on the podium as a medalist at the national tournament.

I came back the next day and the pressure was off me. I won my first two matches to clinch a spot in the top four. Then I lost my last match and finished fourth.

I ran into Corey Arndt from Chadron State again and he beat me again. This time it was 7-4. I just could not beat that guy.

And it was crazy because Chadron was just up the road from where I grew up in western Nebraska.

Even with that setback, it was still a good tournament for me. I became an All-American for the first time and placed in the top four in the country.

I had overcome a lot of adversity, including nearly quitting the sport, to reach this point in my college career.

And I had one more shot to become a national champion.

During that offseason, I trained hard, lifted a lot and I became bigger. I felt really strong going into my senior season at 190 pounds.

I was ranked all year and I was the No. 5 seed going into the 1998 DII national tournament in Pueblo, Colorado.

I advanced to the semifinal round to face Nebraska-Omaha's Jose Medina, who was ranked No. 1 nationally and had won the North Central Conference tournament.

Medina had beaten me twice during the season. He had pinned me both times with a headlock.

Even though he had pinned me twice, mentally I was ready to go. I knew I could do it going into our semifinal match.

In the match at nationals against Medina, I put the legs in and was able to turn him on the edge of the mat and record two near-fall points. I knew I had the match won.

PURPLE REIGN

After a stoppage in the bout, I walked back to the center and said to myself, "I got this. I'm gonna win this."

I ended up winning 5-3. I had advanced to the national championship match.

Sixth-seeded Link Steffen from Southwest Minnesota State tore through the other side of the bracket en route to landing a spot against me in the 190-pound finals.

I think he scouted me pretty well. I made a critical mistake and I gave up some back points.

He reversed me in the second period and caught me on my back. I was in trouble after that. I tried to come back, but it didn't happen.

I lost the match by an 8-1 score.

I was devastated. It hurt – it stung. I had come so far and committed so much time and energy to the sport for so long, and it was over. There was no more wrestling. I knew I was done. It felt horrible.

I didn't achieve what I wanted to in college and the moment was gone. I wasn't going to be a national champion. There was no recourse and no next year.

As most wrestlers will tell you, it's nearly impossible to completely get over or move past a tough loss.

Even guys like Olympic gold medalist Dan Gable still have a hard time talking about tough losses they suffered decades before.

You put so much time, effort and sacrifice into a grueling and demanding sport like wrestling that it's especially difficult when you come so close to achieving a goal but ultimately fall just short.

But as time went on, I gained a much better perspective on how my competitive career ended.

I became old enough or wise enough to realize that the loss, although it haunted me and hurt me for a long time, didn't matter as much as the journey. The time, commitment, discipline, sacrifice and what you learn far outweigh the wins and losses. We competed against so many good Division I teams back then – we wrestled some tough guys. Adams State was a very strong program. We saw the best of the best, and wrestled a tough and challenging schedule.

One of the best wrestlers that I ever faced would go on to excel in international wrestling and mixed martial arts.

I wrestled Daniel Cormier at the Cowboy Open in Wyoming when I was a senior at Adams State and he was a freshman at Colby Community College.

My match with Cormier went into overtime. I took a bad shot and he spun around me and won the match. He was a talented young wrestler, but I still wasn't happy about losing.

Obviously, Cormier went on to have a pretty amazing career.

Cormier was an NCAA runner-up for Oklahoma State before making two Olympic teams and winning a world bronze medal in freestyle wrestling.

He went on to hold Ultimate Fighting Championships world titles at heavyweight and light heavyweight in 2018.

Daniel's done really well in his career, but I'm still not happy that he beat me. I should've won that match.

Like I said, it's tough to completely get over some of those setbacks.

One thing I was able to do was learn and grow and use some of those losses as motivation and inspiration in my career.

My experience as a wrestler, where I endured so many highs and lows, prepared me for what I was about to do next.

CHAPTER 2
STAYING IN COLLEGE

My competitive career was over. And I had wrestled my last match. I graduated from college in 1998 and I was a four-time Academic All-American at Adams State with a 3.6 grade-point average.

I started taking graduate classes the last semester that I wrestled.

The next fall, I student taught while I was a graduate assistant at Adams State.

I was done competing, but I was far from finished with the sport of wrestling.

I joined the coaching staff at Adams State as a graduate assistant.

It was a smooth transition from wrestling to coaching and I immediately knew I had a passion for it.

Coaching provided me with a career path in which I could continue to make an impact in a sport that I loved.

I earned a master's degree in health, physical education and recreation in the summer of 1999.

That same summer, I landed my first full-time coaching job.

I applied for virtually every collegiate job that was open. I was determined to find a job.

I wanted to be a college head coach, even though I knew that would be a difficult job to land for someone my age with little experience.

PURPLE REIGN

My persistence paid off when I was hired as the head wrestling coach by Dakota Wesleyan University in Mitchell, South Dakota.

I had become a college head coach at age 24.

I probably didn't appreciate it as much as I should have, but I was grateful to have the opportunity at such a young age.

It was awesome to be running a college program just a couple of years after I had finished wrestling at that level.

I was so young that I didn't really have much of a blueprint for what I wanted to do or a specific list of goals I wanted to achieve. I just wanted to get in there and coach and wrestle with the kids.

I had very little experience, but I was motivated, excited and fired up to be a college head coach.

I had the energy and expertise to make a difference with the wrestlers that I was going to coach.

I wanted to mimic what I had learned from Coach Jehlicka because that was all I knew. It was a formula that worked and it had worked for me when I was competing.

I was still in my early 20s, but I felt like I was ready to become a college coach. I just needed to gain some experience and it was a learn-as-you-go-situation as a head coach.

I had numerous duties at Dakota Wesleyan, including head wrestling coach, assistant football coach and intramural director. I also taught classes in the physical education department.

That was a typical workload for a coach at a smaller college like Dakota Wesleyan, and I understood that.

It was a lot of work and a lot of hours, even for a young guy fresh out of college. I gained a lot of experience and I learned a lot. It was definitely trial-by-fire. The recruiting process was tough sometimes – sitting in a kid's living room when I was only five years older than him and trying to convince a family to have their son come wrestle for me.

I was at Dakota Wesleyan four seasons from 1999-2003.

One of my wrestlers, Justin Portenier, would go on to have an outstanding college career.

HOW GRAND ISLAND BECAME A NEBRASKA WRESTLING DYNASTY

When I first took the job at Dakota Wesleyan, I knew the first thing I had to do was jump on recruiting. I needed some wrestlers on my roster.

I went back to what was familiar and that was western Nebraska. I started calling coaches that I knew.

I called Dale Hall, who I wrestled for at Alliance High School, and told him I was looking for kids he thought could compete on the college level.

Dale made a recommendation that I'm incredibly grateful for to this day.

"I don't think this Justin Portenier kid from Gering has signed," Dale told me. "I think he's pretty good."

"What do you like about him?" I asked.

"He's a tough, aggressive, hard-nosed kid," Dale replied. "And he pins a lot of people."

Dale was right. Justin wasn't really being recruited by anybody. And he was pretty darn good.

Justin had the dubious distinction of being a guy who lost in the semifinals of the Nebraska state tournament all four years of high school.

He was a heck of a wrestler who fell one match short of walking in the state's Parade of Champions for four straight years.

Portenier placed sixth, fourth, third and third in his four trips to the state tournament.

And I am sure that is part of why Justin flew under the radar in recruiting.

He never made it to the state finals and that motivated him. Justin wanted to prove to people he was better than that.

And the good news was that he still wanted to wrestle, and he was eager for an opportunity to compete in college.

I tracked down Justin's phone number and called him. He agreed to go on a campus visit to Dakota Wesleyan.

Justin had one other offer, from William Penn in Iowa.

I made my recruiting pitch to Justin, and we talked about being from the same part of Nebraska. We had that common bond and that's where I think we had an instant connection.

PURPLE REIGN

I made an offer to him and he accepted. He was my first commit and my first recruit.

Justin was a very dangerous and entertaining wrestler who would drive me crazy at times with his unorthodox style.

He was a wide-open, go-for-broke style wrestler who could end a match in the blink of an eye. He also would take chances and risks at times that might land him in trouble during a match.

And that's what would make me, as his coach, a little crazy.

He made a big impact right away in our lineup at 125 pounds. He was dynamic and goofy, but he was very capable. He was fearless – he would get in there and scrap with anybody. He was pinning people left and right. He had a great spladle, his No. 1 move. He would stick out his leg and bait his opponents to grab it. Then he would lock around them and hook up his spladle.

The spladle is a wrestling technique commonly used as a counter and pinning move to a single-leg takedown attempt.

Once you lock up a spladle, the opposing wrestler has little or no chance to break free from it.

I was more of a fundamental coach and the spladle is considered more of a junk type of move, especially at the collegiate level.

When I first started coaching Justin, I tried to convince him to stop relying on it so much.

I tried to get my message across.

"Quit using garbage and doing that."

But after a year, he kept pinning people with the spladle.

I stopped saying anything about it.

It wasn't garbage if it got the job done.

Justin's pinning power led him to a fourth-place finish as a sophomore at the 2001 NAIA national tournament.

He was becoming a dominant force and he looked like a guy who was a capable of contending for a national title.

A year later, Justin was on a roll. He got hot late in his junior year and carried that into nationals. He was wrestling great and had a ton of confidence going into NAIAs.

He started strong at the two-day national tournament in Great Falls, Montana. He rattled off three straight wins to reach the national championship match in 2002.

After falling short of reaching the finals in his high school career, Justin had finally made the finals of a big tournament.

That was a very big deal to him, but at that point he wasn't settling for just being in the finals.

He wanted to win that national championship.

Justin was the No. 5 seed and he would face No. 2 seed Carl Valley of Montana State-Northern in the NAIA national finals at 125 pounds.

Terry Brands and Lee Fullhart, NCAA Division I champions for Iowa, were at Montana State-Northern coaching as assistants to head coach David Ray that year.

Valley was a very good wrestler who had been a finalist at junior college nationals.

Justin had wrestled Valley early in the season, and was down eight points in the match before he slapped a spladle on Valley to pin him.

Valley was determined not to get spladled again, and he didn't in the rematch.

The whistle blew to start the match in the national finals and Justin went right to work. He baited Valley into a shot, and then Justin tried to work his spladle but it didn't work.

Obviously, he had learned his lesson in the previous match and I'm sure Valley's coaches reminded him of what happened.

After his spladle attempt was stopped, Justin kept wrestling during that sequence and was looking for an opening.

He found one when he scooted around Valley and locked an inside cradle on him.

Valley was in trouble.

Big trouble.

Justin tipped Valley to his back and the referee quickly moved into position before slapping the mat.

Justin Portenier had won the national championship.

He had pinned Valley just 1 minute and 29 seconds into their finals match.

We went crazy, absolutely crazy. It was an incredible moment.

PURPLE REIGN

Justin became the first national champion in our school's history in any sport. It was a very significant moment for Dakota Wesleyan. It was exciting to be a part of that. Justin did an amazing job. He really came through.

And in typical Justin fashion, he won with a dramatic pin in the first period. His matches were never boring.

That will always be one of the highlights of my time as a wrestling coach.

Justin had overcome a lot of adversity, including the near-misses at the high-school level, to become a national champion.

He was a great example of what perseverance and persistence can lead to in a sport like wrestling.

He never stopped chasing his goals and his dreams.

And it paid off for him. In a big, big way.

Justin was an interesting young man to coach. He was very playful and he really liked to joke around. He was a goofy kid who also was very likeable.

I know Justin would joke around a lot to help keep him loose and relaxed before big matches. He would always mess around with my assistant coach, Jay Swatek, before his matches. As a young coach, I was so nervous and jittery before a big match, and Justin helped calm us all down.

One message I think Justin really took to heart was how I would tell him to do nothing different in preparation for any match. That was a lesson I learned in both my high school finals loss and again in my college national finals loss.

I think I learned as much or more from him as he learned from me.

Justin had a tremendous college career at Dakota Wesleyan.

Justin set 11 school records in college, including most wins in a season (31) and a career (94). He also set marks for most falls in a season (19) and in a career (55).

Justin is now a member of the Dakota Wesleyan University Hall of Fame.

After graduating from DWU, he joined the U.S. Army and served in Iraq.

Justin was the right kid at the right time for Dakota Wesleyan. Those were great times, magical times when Justin wrestled for me. He accomplished so much during his time in college.

Justin Portenier will always have a special place in my heart.

All of those kids at Dakota Wesleyan were important to me. I was a young coach and we had a lot of fun trying to build a program together.

We added some other good kids during my time at Dakota Wesleyan. We had a heavyweight named Chad Johnson, who placed seventh in the country at the NAIA level. Chad also played football and he did a great job for us on the wrestling mat.

Chad was probably as much of a "big-move" wrestler as Justin. Chad had a lethal double overhook throw that would morph into a headlock finish. He twice recorded nine-second falls, including one in the national tournament.

My time in South Dakota was rewarding, but it was also very challenging. I learned some tough lessons as a young coach.

Justin Portenier came back as a senior to try and repeat as national champion for us, but he was battling an elbow injury that kept him out of the lineup for much of the season. He had surgery around Thanksgiving time his senior year.

He came back shortly before the regional tournament. He didn't have much practice time, but he somehow made it back to the national championship match.

Justin was a tough kid and a tremendous competitor who knew how to perform when the stakes were highest.

He came up just short in his bid to repeat as a national champion for Dakota Wesleyan.

He lost to a kid from the University of Mary in a close match in the national finals.

Aaron Hartnell of Mary defeated Justin 7-5 in overtime in the NAIA tournament finals at 125 pounds.

I still believe had there been replay available to us then we would have won that match. A good friend of mine, Rick Fink, who officiated at that NAIA national tournament, told me a few times that he believed Justin should have won that match.

PURPLE REIGN

There was a call on the edge of the mat where we felt Justin should have been awarded a takedown. And then Justin gave up a controversial takedown in overtime near the edge of the mat.

It was a good match and I think the outcome could have been different if Justin could've stayed healthy and been on the mat more that season.

It was a heartbreaking way for Justin to finish, but that didn't diminish what he did during his college career.

Justin did an amazing job just to get back to the finals. He was nowhere near 100 percent because of his injury and the time he had been off the mat, but he was a great competitor and he showed that in his final college tournament.

Justin had an outstanding college career. Not bad for a guy who was completely overlooked by almost everybody coming out of high school.

It's crazy to think that our connection to western Nebraska is the reason we convinced him to come wrestle for me in college.

I am very thankful and appreciative of that.

Justin had great success at Dakota Wesleyan. He remained the only national champion in any sport in the school's history up until 2018 when the women's basketball team won the national title.

Brandon Hays, another All-American I coached at DWU, was the younger brother of two of my college teammates, Chuck and Alan Hays. Alan and I had arrived at Adams State at the same time and we graduated together. Chuck was an All-American and graduated when Alan and I were freshman. Brandon came to DWU as a hard-nosed, tough kid and placed eighth the same year Portenier was fourth and Johnson was seventh.

In the years that followed, Jared Digmann and Scott Loveless became All-Americans as well. Both went on to coach – Digmann at Parkston High School and Loveless is still the head coach at Millard North in Omaha after a stint at Omaha Northwest High School.

We were having good success, but I faced more than my share of challenges at Dakota Wesleyan.

I was pretty frustrated in a lot of ways during my time there.

HOW GRAND ISLAND BECAME A NEBRASKA WRESTLING DYNASTY

We didn't have a wrestling room and we didn't have very good facilities. I was looking for more support, but I wasn't getting what I felt we needed so I was applying for other college jobs.

Jeff Tomlin, one of my high school football coaches, had accepted the position of head football coach at Grand Island Senior High back in my home state of Nebraska.

We had been coached in high school by Skip Olds in Alliance. Tomlin was leaving Alliance to move to Grand Island.

Jeff called me in the spring of 2003 and said that the head wrestling position was open at Grand Island. He also wanted me to join his football staff as an assistant coach.

I wasn't overly enthused about taking a high school job after being a college head coach, but felt I needed to change what I was doing. I applied for it and was granted an interview. The facilities at Grand Island were outstanding compared to what I was used to at Dakota Wesleyan.

Just the wrestling room alone was over two full mats and the mats stayed down all year. In the interview, my mind was spinning with the potential that I felt existed. Ultimately, Dr. Kent Mann, the principal, and Joe Kutlas, the athletic director, offered me the job. What they were offering was almost double my salary at Dakota Wesleyan. It was a job I couldn't afford to pass up.

But it was a job I wasn't quite sure that I wanted.

I was offered the job on a Wednesday, the day after I interviewed. I reluctantly turned the offer down on a Thursday, but changed my mind and called back the next day to say I would take it.

I believe Dr. Mann knew I wanted the job and I think he wanted me. He told me to take a couple of days and think about it. I thought about it over the weekend, and I called back on Monday and took the job. I was going to teach English, but taught physical education instead.

My annual salary at Dakota Wesleyan had started at $28,000 when I was coaching two sports, running intramurals and teaching. After being there a couple of years, they cut my salary to $24,000. I was just coaching wrestling at that point along with teaching some courses.

PURPLE REIGN

I was going to make considerably more money by taking a teaching and coaching job at the high school level.

It was tough to say goodbye to college coaching, but the offer at Grand Island was just too good to pass up. I needed to take it.

After my first year at Grand Island, I experienced more good fortune.

I reconnected with the woman who would eventually become my wife.

During my days as a lifeguard in Hemingford, about 20 miles northwest of my hometown of Alliance, I developed a lot of good friendships.

When I was a junior in high school, I started dating a girl from there who was in the same class as a girl named Kelli Koozer.

About a decade later, in 2004, I was coaching football in Grand Island with Kelli's brother, Chris Koozer. Chris is now the head football coach at Sidney High School in western Nebraska.

When I first moved to Grand Island, I asked Chris how his family was doing and I became better acquainted with him. And I was definitely interested in hearing what Kelli was doing.

Kelli and I started talking and we began dating in October 2004.

Kelli was living in Lincoln when we reconnected in 2004. She and her third-grade son had moved to Lincoln from Alliance.

She's always been a hard-working woman with multiple jobs. She was very determined and I was impressed. We had an instant connection and had a lot of fun together.

We had a number of mutual friends back in high school and she knew me from when I was a lifeguard at the pool. But we really didn't know each other that well.

She was an athlete and I remember watching her play sports in high school. She competed in volleyball, basketball and track.

When we started dating, we really hit it off. I was really attracted to her and we just had a great time together. It didn't take long for the relationship to become serious.

We were married the next year, in November 2005.

We now have three sons – Dylan, Caden and Keyan.

CHAPTER 3
BACK TO HIGH SCHOOL

Being a college head coach was a dream of mine and it became a reality for me at a very young age. I loved coaching at the college level, but financially it wasn't working for me.

I had my annual salary at Dakota Wesleyan reduced by $4,000, and after starting my coaching career there, it was time for me to make a change.

It wasn't all about the money – there were some other frustrations I had at Dakota Wesleyan as well. I enjoyed coaching Justin Portenier to the school's first national title and I built some fantastic relationships, but I needed to move on to my next adventure.

When I was hired to teach and coach at Grand Island in 2003, I was making in the mid-$40,000 range annually.

It was almost twice as much as I was making as a college head coach at the NAIA level. It didn't make much sense, but that was the reality.

The good news was I was taking over a wrestling program at Grand Island that was in good shape.

The Islanders had enjoyed their share of success at the state level in Nebraska with two coaches who had led the program for the previous 35 years.

It was a program I was very familiar with. I competed against them numerous times in high school, and I suffered one of my toughest losses there during the district tournament my sophomore year.

PURPLE REIGN

The Islanders had made a significant impact at the state tournament, collecting three top-three finishes in Class A.

Grand Island won its first state team championship in 1973 as four of its wrestlers advanced to the finals under coach Rod Shada. Gary Baldwin captured his first of two straight state championships that year at 138 pounds. Terry Brown, Dan Graves and Dennis Baker each placed second at state for the Islanders in 1973.

Shada was the head coach at Grand Island from 1967-80 and compiled a very respectable 92-42-3 dual meet record.

In addition to his 1973 state championship team, Coach Shada coached eight conference championship teams, one district championship team, three individual state champions and 19 state medalists in the top four.

He was inducted into the Nebraska Scholastic Wrestling Coaches Hall of Fame in 1984 and served as a long-time official for Nebraska high school wrestling.

Kurt Frohling succeeded Shada and led the program for the next 23 seasons from 1980-2003. His teams won 135 dual meets and finished in the top three in the state on two occasions.

Frohling led Grand Island to a second-place state finish in Class A in 1983. The Islanders were third at the state tournament in 1991.

Steve Scott led the 1983 team after reaching the finals before placing second. Grand Island also had medalists in Robert Shinke (fourth), Gus Patsios (fifth), Dan Keck (fifth) and Joe Hostler (fifth).

Hostler followed in 1984 with his own state championship, Frohling's first at Grand Island. Frohling's best years came during the late 1980's into the early 1990's. During those years, the Islanders won four conference and three district team titles. In 1988, Gary Peterson won an individual state title at 189 pounds.

The 1991 Islanders were led by state runner-up finishers Ryan Rathbun and Chad Vokoun. The team also had state medalists that year in Brad Kelly (third), John Morrow (fourth), Brian Kelly (fourth) and Joey Moritz (sixth).

Brian Kelly had won a Class A state championship at 145

pounds in 1990. Morrow won state for Grand Island at 119 pounds in 1993.

Efrain Ayala was the school's next state champion, winning a Class A crown at 135 pounds in 2003.

He went on to become an NCAA Division II qualifier for Minnesota State-Mankato and is now the head coach at the University of Wisconsin-Oshkosh.

Frohling was inducted into the Nebraska Scholastic Wrestling Coaches Association Hall of Fame in 2004.

My two predecessors, Shada and Frohling, were still at Grand Island High School when I took over as head coach. They were both still employed at the school. Rod was working as a counselor and Kurt was a science teacher.

Kurt was still the sophomore football coach when I got there and we actually coached football together.

I asked Kurt if he would be interested in helping me out with wrestling after I had been there a few years.

What could have been a very difficult position for me as a younger coach turned out to be a fantastic position to be in. I had two of the biggest and most familiar fans of the program cheering for me and the kids in Coach Shada and Coach Frohling.

It was great having the former coaches around. They were very supportive and they knew the kids.

We would talk wrestling, and I had a great relationship with both of those guys.

They never told me what to do or how to do it – they just provided support and they were the biggest fans of the team.

I remember on competition days I would be teaching and one period Coach Shada would stop by my classroom to talk about the dual and map out the team score. Then I would get to do it again from another perspective during Coach Frohling's planning period.

They wanted the program to excel and it was awesome to have their interest and support. That meant a great deal to me.

Grand Island still had a strong program when I took over as head coach in 2003. In Coach Frohling's final season during the 2002-03 school year, his team had five state medalists with Ayala capturing his state championship. They tied for 10th place in the Class A standings with 75.5 points.

But it had been a while since Grand Island had been in contention to win a state team title.

I considered the program a sleeping giant when I arrived there in the fall of 2003.

There was the potential there for us to be a state championship contender in Class A.

I felt like the dynamics of the community were in place to build a championship program. Grand Island is a very blue collar, tough, hard-working town. I felt like those were the types of kids that enjoyed the sport of wrestling and would fit in well with our program.

The youth programs were thriving at that time. There were a lot of kids to pick from in terms of building a program. It felt like there was a lot of potential.

I also had some very good coaches with strong credentials at the middle schools, and that was very important for us. We had good people in place who could help develop these young wrestlers and lay a foundation for high school wrestling. A lot of the components were already in place for us to be successful.

There was a good talent base at Grand Island.

Winning state was definitely on my mind when I started coaching there.

My five-year plan included winning a state championship at Grand Island.

I remember a conversation that I had with Aurora's Bill Wofford, one of the state's most respected coaches. Bill told me that you can see significant change in a college program in 2-3 years. In high school, he said it takes 4-6 years to really implement your program.

I knew right away that there were areas in which we could make improvements.

Technically, we needed to improve. I wanted to implement more of a collegiate style of wrestling that I felt was more conducive to my coaching philosophy.

I also thought our conditioning needed to get better.

In addition, I was infusing my philosophies into the team. It was a pretty big transition when I came in there, and I know it wasn't easy for the wrestlers.

I also wanted to make sure the youth clubs and middle schools were doing everything they could to prepare the kids for the high school level. That's critical in building a top-level program. When building a great high school program, you have to make sure you are building a streamlined K-12 program. Teaching the same techniques and philosophies all the way through is vital.

The changes were a little bit difficult for some, but most of the kids jumped on board. The changes were toughest on the class of seniors during my first year. It was a big adjustment for them and a bit of a struggle because there were a lot of changes right before their senior year. They had done things a certain way for a lot of years and then had to adapt.

Just the fact that it was different was the toughest adjustment for them, having a new head coach in their last year of high school. I knew first-hand as Dale Hall came to Alliance prior to my senior year.

Coach Frohling had been there for almost 25 years – his culture was deeply rooted in the kids and the families of the wrestlers. I understood why it was difficult for them, but I thought it was necessary to implement my changes.

Two of the kids I appreciated most for their leadership and work ethic were Jake Reinert and Jared Williams. Both made a lot of sacrifices as seniors and both did well through the transition. Their leadership made everything much easier for me.

We started doing a lot of hard drilling in practice. We also did some film study. They hadn't done much of that in the past. I didn't watch hours and hours of tape, but the film study was helpful. I could show a wrestler something on video to help them learn from a mistake or to see what an opponent was doing.

We had some kids really latch on and buy into what we were doing my first year, and that was huge for us.

And I had to buy into what we were doing after going from

the college level to a high school program.

Once I made the decision to come to Grand Island, I was fully committed. There was no turning back after I left Dakota Wesleyan.

I was the head wrestling coach at Grand Island. I had a plan and a blueprint, which was very different from when I started at Dakota Wesleyan. I had some experience as a head coach, and I jumped in with both feet and went right to work.

I had excellent administrative support as well.

Dr. Mann, our principal, and Tom Kruger, our assistant principal, had been collegiate athletes and former wrestling coaches. Cindy Wells, another assistant principal, had been a head volleyball coach.

There were a lot of sports-minded people who were incredibly supportive of me and what I was there to do.

A number of them had been involved in wrestling, so they had a great understanding of my role as a head coach.

My first year as the head coach at Grand Island, we finished 10th at state and had four state medalists. Brandon Hudiburgh placed third and Logan Hayman was fourth with Jake Reinert and Eric Wieland each finishing fifth.

It was frustrating that first year. My first couple of years at Grand Island were challenging. We were letting some matches get away.

We wanted to wrestle aggressively, attack and pin people. I was infusing a mentality of dominating our opponents.

I had high expectations for the kids and the program at Grand Island.

My practices have always been intense. We ran two mornings a week in addition to our regular practices after school. The kids also had weight training classes.

We were always working hard and putting the time in.

We started going to more camps in the spring and summer. It started to become part of our culture to wrestle year-round, but it didn't happen overnight.

The extra time on the mat made a huge difference for us.

HOW GRAND ISLAND BECAME A NEBRASKA WRESTLING DYNASTY

In those early years, the quality of freestyle and Greco-Roman wrestling in Nebraska weren't as good as it is now or had been when I was growing up. There has been a nice resurgence in recent years.

We wrestled a lot of folkstyle in the spring and summer.

I started a wrestling league. We would bring college coaches in as technicians to Grand Island to work with the kids.

I coached my first individual state champions the next two seasons. Caleb Tyler won a Class A state title at heavyweight in 2005 before Brandon Hudiburgh followed by winning state at 189 pounds in 2006.

Caleb moved into Grand Island as a senior. He had moved around a lot, and he had been at Omaha Burke and Elkhorn high schools. He didn't have much stability in his home life.

He was extremely explosive and athletic. He was a 6-foot, 250-pound kid that was just raw. I coached him in football and got to know him really well during the fall.

Caleb was very talented and more athletic than most heavyweights. He came in and made a huge impact. I wrestled with him a lot. He was the first real superstar that I had at Grand Island, although we knew we had a few more studs coming up through our youth program.

I wish I would've had Caleb for a few more years.

He was a nice addition to our team and he did a great job that season.

Caleb edged Ricky Henry from Omaha Burke 3-1 in the state finals in 2005. Henry went on to win state the next year. Henry became a standout lineman for the University of Nebraska before going on to play in the National Football League.

Caleb was an undefeated state champion at heavyweight. He was a tremendous athlete and a great kid. It was a really good, physical match with Henry – Caleb did a great job. He controlled the match and won a state title.

It was a great moment to coach a state champion in the same building where I had won my state title a little over 10 years before. It also was the last year the Nebraska School Activities Association

PURPLE REIGN

held the state tournament at the University of Nebraska's Devaney Center in Lincoln.

That was a big year for us. Hayman and Hudiburgh also made the finals. Both wrestlers placed second.

We finished fifth in the state in Class A in 2005, scoring 102 points. We had a nice team that year and we were making progress.

Brandon's older brother, Harold Hudiburgh Jr., kept me from the state tournament my sophomore year. He beat me at districts in February 1991 in Grand Island.

It was a horrible experience losing that match, and it was a tough spill to swallow. I was seeded third going into the district tournament.

I knew right away when I came to Grand Island that Brandon's older brother had beaten me when I was in high school.

Brandon was a sophomore when I arrived in Grand Island and I became his coach. He placed third at state my first year at GISH.

Brandon was an explosive wrestler for a big kid. He was a stud. He was athletic, he was aggressive. He was a tough kid who had three older brothers, an older sister and a younger brother. They were a very tight-knit family. He was the most athletic boy of the family. He was strong and powerful and had a little mean streak to him.

He was tough as nails, but as tough as Brandon was, he was really great with kids. I remember taking my stepson on trips with us and Brandon was always really good to Dylan.

During that time Brandon and a few other kids were borderline mean to some kids, but I thought it was great how he was just a big kid to some of the younger kids around the program.

In Brandon's junior year, he took it another step farther and reached the state finals against Josh Marcum of Omaha Benson.

Marcum came out and took Brandon down with a fireman's carry and pinned him in the first period.

Brandon came back strong and was pretty dominant his senior year. He was ranked second all year behind Marcum.

Hudiburgh and Marcum both advanced to the state championship match again the following season in 2006.

The finals bout was a rematch of the 171-pound title bout when Marcum had pinned Hudiburgh in 2005.

Both wrestlers had bumped up a class to 189 pounds in 2006. Marcum rolled to a 16-1 win by technical superiority over Hudiburgh in the district finals just a week before they would meet again.

He got handled. Marcum was an impressive wrestler and athlete. He took Brandon down with three or four different takedowns. I watched the film of that match after districts and Marcum put on a clinic.

He hit a single, a fireman's carry and a high crotch. He attacked both sides of the body.

I wasn't sure how we were going to stop the guy.

I wanted to figure out what his top takedown was and try to take that away from him. Since he was able to score in several different ways, I was kind of resigned to the fact that we weren't going to beat him.

I just didn't know if it was possible.

Brandon wasn't a technical wrestler. He was a brawler and a big-move pinner. Coming up with a strategic game plan against Marcum wasn't a great option.

I wrestled with Brandon a lot that year. I remember thinking I needed to throw several different attacks at him on Monday the week of state. Then Tuesday and Wednesday, I just came at Brandon hard, but let him win most positions to help build his confidence. I really felt like our best chance was to help build him up and allow him to believe he could do it.

I told Brandon to throw everything he had at him and not to hold back.

He was a senior and he had nothing to lose.

It was the first year for the state tournament at the Qwest Center in Omaha, and I walked out onto the floor with Brandon before the finals.

I put my arm around him, looked up into the stands and glanced around in the sparkling new arena and delivered a message to him.

PURPLE REIGN

"Brandon, there is probably not a single person in this building who thinks you can win the match," I told him matter-of-factly. "But the only thing that matters is what you think in your head."

Even with the pep talk, I wasn't convinced that Brandon could do it, but I knew I had to show him I believed in him.

I walked away from the conversation thinking I was one of the people who didn't think he could win, but I knew stranger things had happened.

And the improbable did happen.

Brandon went out there and did a tremendous job. It was an incredible turnaround. Brandon beat Marcum 6-5 in the state finals.

He pulled off a huge upset.

Brandon was able to ride Marcum and take something out of him. I don't think Marcum had wrestled a whole six-minute match all year. It eventually took its toll on him.

In the third period, we had a one-point lead and Marcum reversed Brandon.

Then very late in the match, Brandon reversed Marcum to take the lead. He rode him out to win the match.

Brandon Hudiburgh had won a state title.

It was a fantastic moment because of how heavily the odds were stacked against him. He was my second state champion.

A big part of coaching is manipulating an athlete's mind. It didn't matter what I thought – I wasn't going out on the mat with him. The work had been done and he was as prepared as I could get him.

It was up to him to perform and he did the job. It was mayhem – it was a blur when he won.

My assistant coach, Geoff Cyboron, and I were so tense as we watched the final seconds tick off the clock.

Brandon ran over and jumped into my arms. There was a great shot of him in the Grand Island newspaper from that magical moment. I remember jubilation and shock. I couldn't believe it, but he did.

Everybody was cheering. Marcum took his singlet straps down and threw his headgear 10 rows into the stands. I'm sure he was disappointed.

It is kind of surreal that Brandon won that match. But he really stepped up and delivered.

He was a huge underdog, but you've always got a shot when you go out there. He had every right to win it as much as Marcum did. I knew it was possible. I just didn't think it was going to happen.

Brandon had the ability to wrestle with anybody. He had pinned Sonny Yohn of Alamosa, Colorado a couple of times in matches during the summer. Sonny also beat Brandon a few times before he went on to become an All-American for the University of Minnesota. But Brandon did show he had that kind of potential against competition of that caliber.

Brandon Hudiburgh's magical moment at state almost didn't happen.

Brandon fell asleep where we had our camp set up outside the weigh-in area that morning and he wasn't in the room at the start of weigh-ins.

Brandon ran in a little late and his weight class was in line. Marcum actually helped him sneak in to get in line to weigh in. That's crazy to think that Marcum, whom he would upset in the finals, was the guy who helped him.

Brandon went on to excel at the college level.

He earned NAIA All-American honors for Hastings College at 197 pounds in 2008. He placed fifth at the national tournament and was named Great Plains Athletic Conference Wrestler of the Year.

Two years after Brandon's huge upset win, I watched another wrestler follow an unlikely path at state when Isaiah Aguilar qualified at 112 pounds.

Isaiah came to us through Jeff Westerby's work as the counselor and head wrestling coach at Walnut Middle School in Grand Island. Walnut was a school with many low-income students and a high minority population. Westerby was a major force in getting kids out for wrestling and transitioning them to high school.

I was fortunate to work with Isaiah. He was a very quiet, introverted kid who was talented, athletic and a good scrambler.

I always felt his biggest hurdle to overcome was his lack of

PURPLE REIGN

belief in himself.

Isaiah ran into Tim Crocker from Kearney in the state semis. He had struggled in previous bouts against Crocker. It was a good, close match. In the closing seconds of the match, in desperation, Isaiah hit a duck under and pulled him down for a takedown for a 4-3 win. He had lost to Crocker seven times before that match.

He pulled out a dramatic last-second win and landed a spot in the state championship match.

That win gave Isaiah a huge confidence boost and helped him believe that he could win against the best guys in the state.

It wasn't a lack of ability or talent, he just had to go out there and do it.

I had to help him believe.

He did it in the semis, why not do it again in the finals?

He just needed positive reinforcement.

Isaiah would face another nemesis, Patrick Rollins of Omaha Creighton Prep, in the 2008 state finals.

Rollins was a stud. He had won state the year before, and he had pinned Isaiah early in the year in a dual. Isaiah wrestled him again in the district finals and he got tech-falled by a 16-1 score.

Isaiah was beat up physically. He had tears in his eyes after the match. He had been manhandled by a very good wrestler. Rollins was a prodigy and he was destined to do great things. He was coached by Tim Neumann, who had been the long-time head coach at the University of Nebraska.

Going into the rematch at state, we took more of a technical approach. We kept teaching Isaiah how to defend those shots and use his scrambling ability.

But just like Brandon Hudiburgh had done two years before, Isaiah needed to believe those losses didn't matter and I reminded him of that during a pre-match pep talk.

"Just open up and let yourself go," I told him. "Dude, you're so athletic. Use it to your advantage."

Isaiah did just that, countering shot attempts by Rollins to score the first and the last takedown of the bout.

With the match deadlocked 4-4, time was running out.

Isaiah defended a leg attack by diving off, grabbing Rollins' leg, rolling through and coming out the back door to score a takedown with 30 seconds left.

It was a beautifully executed move.

Isaiah then kept him on the mat, riding him out and achieving the stunning upset win.

I don't know how Isaiah did it. It's hard to have confidence wrestling against a guy who pinned you and teched you. I try to empower kids to believe in themselves. It was such an oddly similar situation to Brandon. He believed he could do it and he did it. It was an amazing moment.

Isaiah believed he could do it and he won a state championship. He opened up that one weekend and really blossomed when it counted the most.

It was incredible to see him wrestle like he was capable to win a state title.

He saved his best matches for the right moment at the right time.

Those memories of Brandon and Isaiah are priceless.

Those are the moments as a coach I hold so close to my heart.

The kids did it and they deserve the credit. I'm very proud to have played a part in helping them achieve their goals.

I hope I opened the door for them to compete and perform at their best when the stakes were the highest.

Brandon and Isaiah went out there and performed when most people didn't think they could do it. They both beat returning state champions.

It is really unheard of what they did, especially under the circumstances.

I always wanted my athletes to believe in themselves even if I had to manipulate them into believing it. My greatest wish for all, but especially those two, was that those moments and the lessons that made them possible would help them in their lives after wrestling.

They are extraordinary moments I will never forget and I'm sure they won't either.

CHAPTER 4
BREAKING THROUGH

We started the 2008-09 season believing we had a legitimate chance to make a run at the Class A state wrestling championship. My plan had Grand Island winning state by my fifth season.

We didn't quite make it. We took fourth in the 2008 state tournament in Class A with a strong performance in Year 5, but we wanted more.

Much more.

We were ready to make a run at a championship during my sixth season coaching the Islanders.

Millard South had a four-year stranglehold on Class A. Everybody wanted to beat them. We were the up-and-coming team in Nebraska.

We had a lot of medalists returning with an influx of excellent young talent coming in. There was a lot of hope and excitement. We knew we had a chance to do something special. We just didn't know how special.

I had very high expectations for our team and our program. But even with the optimism, I couldn't have envisioned what we were about to accomplish.

Perennial power Millard South was the team to beat. We knew they were the No. 1 program in Class A.

I would remind the kids about it all the time during practice.

PURPLE REIGN

"I know Millard South is training really hard right now," I called out to my team. "If you want to beat them, you have to outwork them."

We used that as motivation on a daily basis. We were excited and fired up to have that opportunity to compete against a team of their caliber.

We also were very excited about a great freshman class that we had coming in. We couldn't wait to get that group of talented younger wrestlers on the mat.

Before we would battle Millard South, we received a tough early test in December when we hosted the Flatwater Fracas. It was a multi-state dual tournament in Grand Island that attracted top-flight teams from Nebraska and beyond.

Prior to the 2008 event, we received a request from Billings Skyview High School in Montana to join the event. I was all for adding them. Their coach was the father of Joey and Ty Malia, twins who had wrestled for the University of Nebraska. I connected with their father because of that.

We were excited, and this was always my vision for the event – to attract national and regional top teams. At the time of the event, Amateur Wrestling News had Skyview ranked in their top 40 high school programs nationally. We knew they would be a formidable opponent, but it was what our event and our program needed.

That year a fairly substantial snowstorm was hitting the area on Thursday, the day before the Fracas was set to begin, and left several teams unable to attend. Nonetheless, the show went on. Several teams missed Friday's matches, but arrived on Saturday. During the regular event, we won every dual by a landslide right up to the final-round matchup with nationally ranked Skyview. The entire arena was focused on this match against the two teams that dominated all of their previous duals.

The dual started at 119 pounds. Skyview won by fall and we responded with back-to-back major decisions to push ahead 8-6. Skyview would win 5 of the next 6 matches and took a commanding lead of 33-11 going into the 189-pound match. It didn't look good for us, but we were heading into a powerful portion of our

HOW GRAND ISLAND BECAME A NEBRASKA WRESTLING DYNASTY

lineup and finishing with two strong freshman lightweights. Before the freshmen came to the mat, three strong juniors pulled us back into the dual with three straight falls. Alan Taylor (189), Nate Westerby (215) and Jesse Janulewicz (heavyweight) all delivered with pins for Grand Island. After the succession of pins, we had cut Skyview's seemingly insurmountable lead to 33-29.

Freshman phenom Andrew Riedy won by decision at 103 to pull us within one point and Blake Fruchtl won by a 12-0 major decision at 112 to seal the win for us.

It was an amazing win and everybody was going crazy celebrating, hugging and high-fiving after our incredible come-from-behind victory. We began to realize what sort of team we had.

We had knocked off a nationally ranked team and we were off and running during the 2008-09 season.

The arrival of Andrew Riedy coincided with a historic run by the Grand Island Senior High program.

We carried our momentum into the 2009 state tournament in downtown Omaha.

We were on the verge of turning in one of the most dominant performances in state tournament history.

Riedy (103 pounds), Blake Fruchtl (112), Alec Chanthapatheth (130) and Nathan Westerby (215) each captured state titles for Grand Island in 2009.

I knew Riedy and Fruchtl were going to be superstars. We had a bunch of studs in that freshman class.

Carlos Rodriguez was another of our top wrestlers in that freshman class.

We had state finalists in the first three weight classes that year with Riedy (103), Fruchtl (112) and Rodriguez (119). Carlos placed second that year at state.

Riedy was undefeated as a freshman. He went 44-0.

Andrew's father, Rob, was one of our coaches. Rob did a great job for us and Andrew was well-prepared when he stepped onto the mat for his first varsity match.

Andrew was just so technically sound. He was in all the right positons at all the right times.

PURPLE REIGN

He was a crazy tilting fool. He would chop his opponent's arm, trap the guy's wrist on his belt and execute a roll-through tilt. He did it to everyone. It was like clockwork. And he perfected it.

Andrew teched a lot of kids with that. And he pinned a lot of kids with the tilt.

It was definitely his weapon of choice. And the biggest difference-maker in his early high school wrestling.

His formula for success was simple. Takedown and tilt. Nobody could stop him.

His opponents naturally figured out that his tilt was coming, so they developed game plans and strategies to try and stop him. But they didn't work. Andrew, as many great wrestlers do, figured out how to get to his best stuff even when opponents knew it was coming.

Andrew continued to do the tilt and continued to excel. He found different ways to set it up, and he got better and better with the technique.

Andrew advanced to the state finals his freshman year, where he defeated Brittney Taylor of Omaha North 6-2 in the 103-pound finals in Class A.

Taylor was the highest-finishing girl in Nebraska state history while wrestling mainly against boys. She remains the highest female finisher in the history of the state tournament.

We knew this would be a different match for Andrew. There was a lot of media attention on the match with a female reaching the finals.

Andrew handled the situation with poise, as he always did during his career. He had wrestled Brittney before. This time, in the state finals, Andrew controlled the entire match and won it outright.

Andrew Riedy had won his first state title. And taken the first big step in his quest toward history.

Shortly after Andrew's hand was raised, his freshman teammate took the mat for the 112-pound finals.

Blake Fruchtl was another highly touted wrestler who had also been outstanding during his freshman season.

I remember watching Blake in a summer camp prior to his

freshman year in which he had knocked off a Nebraska state champion, Shawn Nagel from Kimball, in a match that wasn't close.

Blake not only beat Nagel, he destroyed him. He beat him handily and just dominated the match. That opened my eyes. It was the summer before Blake started high school. We were excited to see him wrestle for Grand Island Senior High.

Nagel was an excellent wrestler, so we were really impressed when Blake beat him. Nagel went on to win three state titles and became a starter for the University of Nebraska.

Blake had his hands full in his first trip to the state tournament. He earned a 2-1 overtime win over Millard South's Jacob Miller in the 112-pound finals.

It was a tight match. Blake showed good composure in the finals, and he was able to pull out a hard-fought victory. We rolled the dice and put Blake on top in the ultimate overtime, and he was able to ride Miller out for the win.

The purple parade of finalists continued for us in the 119-pound championship bout.

Our third freshman finalist, Carlos Rodriguez, then dropped a 10-6 decision to Omaha Central's Tyrell Galloway in the 119 finals.

Carlos really put it together in the postseason and wrestled well at the state tournament. Our freshmen lightweights had placed first, first and second at state. That was exciting to see and a great sign for the years that would follow.

It was awesome to have so many guys wrestling on that Saturday afternoon in downtown Omaha. We put half of our lineup in the finals that year.

Alec Chanthapatheth was our next state finalist at 130 pounds. Alec went unbeaten during his junior season and won his first state title.

He was a pure athlete. He was flexible and he was difficult to score on. He an ultra-athletic wrestler.

Alec caught onto the sport quickly. He didn't start wrestling until he was in middle school.

Jeff Westerby was one of our coaches who found a lot of those

PURPLE REIGN

tough kids on our championship teams.

Jeff kept many kids out of trouble by putting them on the wrestling team at the middle school. Alec was one of them.

Alec defeated Ethan Fletcher of Omaha Central 5-4 in the state finals.

Alec beat a tough kid. He didn't wrestle his best match that day, but he held in there to get it done.

He had some issues off the mat that spring after the season and was eventually dismissed from the school.

Alec came back and placed fifth at the National Senior High School tournament.

He originally signed with Nebraska-Kearney before ending up at Hastings College.

Alec went on to become a three-time NAIA national qualifier for Hastings. He fell one match short of being an All-American every year.

He had all of the ability in the world. When he wrestled, it was poetry in motion. He would get into bad positions and fluidly wrestle himself out of it like he meant to do it.

He stuck it out and earned his college degree. I'm proud of how Alec turned his life around. He is headed in the right direction.

Nate Westerby became our fourth and final state champion for Grand Island in 2009.

He had twice medaled at the state tournament prior to making the finals.

Nate was another star we could see coming in middle school. He was an athletic, big kid who could attack high and attack low. He wrestled like a technical 160-pounder at 215.

He rolled through his junior year to win the state championship at 215.

Nate pinned Adam Kerr of Lincoln Pius X in the first period in the finals.

Nate scored a solid takedown and then hooked up an inside cradle to win by fall. He was a dominant force that year and it was an awesome way for him to cap his season.

Nate's dad was one of our coaches and he had spent a lot of

time working with him.

I worked with Nate quite a bit and wrestled with him a lot. I pushed him and challenged him. I made him earn it when we wrestled in the room. I didn't want to make it easy for him.

Nate also ended up wrestling for Hastings College.

We finished with 12 state medalists, seven finalists and four champions during that magical 2008-09 season. It was an incredible performance by our kids. They were a dedicated group and it really paid off for them.

We were motivated to knock off Millard South and that was a goal that pushed our kids that entire season.

We would never replicate that season again. I wanted to. I thought we had the talent and ability to do it. We just never quite reached that level again.

We were very, very hungry and very, very motivated that year.

One of those 2009 finalists we had was a kid who made a huge impact in our program's quest to become the best in the state.

Riley Allen placed second in the state at 152 pounds that season. He advanced to the finals before falling to Nick Rimpley of Kearney 6-3 in the state championship match.

Riley was a senior that year. He was one of the few seniors we had on the 2009 team.

Riley was a two-time medalist going into that year. He previously placed fifth and fourth at the state tournament.

He was the quintessential hard-working kid who completely bought into what we were doing. He was the leader that every coach wants. He was a very diligent worker and relentless in the practice room. And he was a vocal leader.

He was the type of athlete that every coach dreams about working with. He was a veteran and he was older, and he led by example.

When he called people out for not working hard or training hard, it was coming with some backing.

The kids looked up to him and he played a huge role with the success that we had.

Riley taught those young kids how to practice and how to

PURPLE REIGN

train.

I can't emphasize enough how important Riley was to the success of our team.

Kids like that are priceless.

Riley took his lumps early in his career and then really progressed. He stuck with it. And then he passed it on to the younger guys.

Riley was a quiet, naïve kid coming into high school. He really improved and developed for us – he did an excellent job.

Right before districts his senior year, Riley broke a bone in his hand. It was a clean break.

He kept his spirits up and told me, "I'm going to fight through it and I'm going to wrestle."

His only loss before districts came in a match where a questionable call went against him. He easily could've been undefeated going into the postseason.

The doctors let Riley wrestle and we had his hand taped up and protected.

After he weighed in at districts, he was given a shot in his hand. It helped numb his hand and alleviate the pain when he competed.

Riley walked up to me with a big smile on his face right before the start of districts.

"I'm ready to go, Coach," Riley said. "I'm ready to wrestle."

He had missed most of the week of practice, but I knew Riley was tough enough to advance to state.

Riley advanced to the district finals and then we pulled him out of the tournament. He had qualified for state. He didn't need to wrestle another match with a broken hand that day.

When we went to Omaha for the state tournament, he did the same thing. He was given a shot in his hand before he would compete.

In the state finals against the kid from Kearney, it seemed like whatever Riley tried to do it somehow went wrong for him.

Riley lost a tough match in the finals. His hand was numb from the shot, but Riley still wasn't 100 percent. He did his best, like he always did for us.

If he would've won the match, we would've broken Omaha Skutt's all-class scoring record by half a point.

It still breaks my heart that Riley lost that match because the kid gave so much to our program. I wish he could've been healthy when he wrestled at state.

That was a tough one. He did such a great job for us that it hurt to see him come so close to winning a state title and come up short.

He didn't win an individual title, but he was very much the leader on the team that won a state championship that year.

Riley went on to wrestle in college at Nebraska-Kearney.

He was just such a great kid. He meant a lot to our program. I can't thank him enough for all that he did for us.

Alan Taylor also was a runner-up for us that season. He placed second at 189 pounds. He also was second the next season in 2010.

Alan was tough, rugged and mean, and he was a brawler when he stepped onto the mat to wrestle.

He caught a bad break when he was illegally slammed in the state semifinals during a match against Nick Mizaur of Omaha Creighton Prep. Alan was awarded the win because the referee determined he had been injured by an illegal move by his opponent.

Alan was thrown on his head and was knocked out cold. It was a very scary few moments after it happened. He suffered a concussion, so he had to forfeit his finals match the next day against Morgan Denson of Millard South.

It was unfortunate that he didn't get a chance to wrestle for the state title, but he wasn't physically able to compete.

Alan did a really good job for us – he was a tough, hard-nosed kid. He would lock up and throw people.

Matt Sedivy was another person who played a huge role for us during my first state championship season at Grand Island.

Matt was from my hometown of Alliance. He was a Class B state runner-up at 140 pounds in 2001.

He wrestled at 149 and 157 pounds for me at Dakota Wesleyan. He was a strong, athletic kid who wrestled with a lot of grit and toughness.

PURPLE REIGN

There is no doubt in my mind that Matt would've been a collegiate All-American if he had stayed healthy. He had shoulder issues that really held him back. He was an excellent wrestler.

In 2008, I recruited Matt to take an elementary physical education job at Grand Island and become my assistant coach.

He was with me for one season and it was during our record-setting state championship season during the 2008-09 school year.

Matt was a young coach who could get in the room and scrap with the kids. The kids loved him. I had a great staff of assistants, but having Matt was awesome for our team. He pushed the kids and drove them.

He was a middleweight so he was able to wrestle with a lot of our kids.

He made a huge impact with our kids.

Matt bridged the gap a lot between the kids and me. He was only 25 years old at the time.

He was with me for one year and then he took over as the head coach at Dakota Wesleyan. He had the same job that I had to start my coaching career.

Matt did a really great job for us and really made a difference for us that season.

A turning point during that championship season occurred during a big mid-season dual against the reigning state champions.

Millard South beat us in a dual meet at their place in mid-January. I learned an important lesson in that dual from how their coach, Doug Denson, adjusted his lineup against us. Coach Denson was very good at looking at matchups and figuring out a way to win a close dual meet.

That loss turned out to be a huge blessing for us. We really came back strong from that. We used that as a motivational tool. We constantly reminded the kids we needed to wrestle lights out at the state tournament to beat Millard South. The kids were really focused when we arrived in Omaha for the 2009 state tournament.

That focus was on full display as Grand Island won its second state title in school history. The first crown came in 1973 when Gary Baldwin won his first of two individual state titles for the

HOW GRAND ISLAND BECAME A NEBRASKA WRESTLING DYNASTY

Islanders.

Our team was really clicking from the very first whistle on Thursday at the 2009 state meet.

Our kids were extremely motivated that year – it was the most motivated team I ever coached. The kids were always ready to work. It was a fantastic year. They really pushed each other and fed off each other. It was an exciting year. We won state by over 100 points. Our team just caught fire. It was one of the largest margins of victory in state history. Our guys had a mindset of dominating their opponents.

Our kids were focused and locked in. They did everything we asked them to and it paid off.

The state title was clinched on Day 2 of the three-day tournament.

I looked at my phone on Friday night on the way back to the hotel and checked the team scoring.

This was what I saw on the screen:

Class A Team Standings
Grand Island 211.5, Millard South 117, Kearney 101

That put a huge smile on my face. We had put seven wrestlers in the finals. And we had already surpassed 200 points with plenty of chances to add to that total on the final day of the tournament on Saturday.

We had a miniature celebration when we returned to the hotel on Friday night, knowing we had locked up the state championship.

I gathered the team and delivered a message to them late Friday night:

"Tomorrow, I want each individual to wrestle for themselves. You get to be selfish and wrestle for yourself to achieve your goals. All that matters to me is that you to go out there and wrestle as well as you possibly can for yourselves."

To nobody's surprise, our kids went out and wrestled well on the last day of the season. They won 4-of-7 finals matches on Saturday.

That performance enabled us to break the Class A state scoring record. We finished with 252.5 points in 2009. Millard South

PURPLE REIGN

was a distant second with 145.5 points.

I had high expectations going into the final weekend, but our team's performance in Omaha exceeded those expectations.

The 252.5 points remains the Class A state tournament record. The 12 state placewinners remain tied for the all-class tournament record.

Our list of state medalists in 2009 also included Matt Rice (third at 135 pounds), Mike Bolan (fourth at 125), Beau Jepson (fifth at 160), Cory Frankenberg (fifth at 285) and Coleman Westerby (sixth at 171).

We had so many kids who contributed that year. It was a total team effort.

Our kids were absolutely on a mission and they were not going to be denied. We were full throttle that whole year with a goal of giving it everything we could. That was the attitude that this team had – they were determined that they were going to do it.

It was such a driven group. And such a pleasure and an honor to coach them.

Another celebration was held when our team returned home to Grand Island.

That state title was a really big deal for our school and our community. There was a big pep rally in front of the whole school. It filled the gym with around 2,500 people showing up to honor the team. It was an amazing turnout and a great show of support.

It was an awesome and incredible experience. We even received rings.

The Grand Island Islanders were the Nebraska state wrestling champions in Class A.

And our athletes were recognized for what they had accomplished.

We had so much fun that year, but we were far from finished.

We were ready to do it.

CHAPTER 5
BACK-TO-BACK

Grand Island entered the 2009-10 wrestling season as the reigning Class A state champions in Nebraska. And we were the favorites to repeat.

There were lofty expectations for that season, but I don't remember feeling pressure to repeat. We reset in March of 2009 and went right back to work. We did all of the offseason work we had done in previous seasons. We lost a couple of good kids from 2009, but we had most of our team back and more tough freshmen coming in from our kids' club.

We had built a culture of high expectations. I also reminded our team that it was not going to be easy to repeat as state champions.

To me, it was about how good we could make our kids. What improvements could we make to perform at our best? I knew the previous year would be very difficult to replicate, but it came down to improvements for everyone in the program.

We wanted to create a challenge to do even better the next season.

We wanted to stay in the national rankings.

We wanted to one up it and do better. That was my mindset and my approach.

We were nationally ranked in 2009. We wrestled Billings Skyview in the Flatwater Fracas in Grand Island. They were nationally ranked when we beat them.

PURPLE REIGN

We were ranked in the top 40 nationally by Amateur Wrestling News. We were in the bottom 10 of the top 40. That was really great for us and an important step for our program in gaining notoriety and credibility.

We were also nationally ranked by WIN Magazine and InterMat. It was great recognition for our kids and for our program.

People outside of Nebraska had taken notice of what we were doing. And that was great to see.

Our kids had worked hard and were reaping the benefits.

I delivered a strong message to our team before the 2009-10 season:

"Let's see if we can do more. We're going to be in tournaments tougher than our state tournament, so we have to work harder. We are going to wrestle some really good teams."

We changed, and upgraded, our schedule. We needed to challenge our team and give them an opportunity to compete against some of the best high school programs in the country.

We added the Top of the Rockies tournament in Colorado to our schedule. It was a really tough tournament with some outstanding teams.

The best teams from Colorado were there along with some of the best teams from Wyoming, New Mexico and Texas.

We went to The Clash in Rochester, Minnesota. The Clash is a massive dual-meet event held right after Christmas. Teams come in from all over the country to compete.

We were excited and honored to be invited to compete in The Clash, but the weather wasn't cooperating the day we were supposed to travel.

A long trip to Minnesota became even longer. And more nerve-wracking.

We drove though snow and ice, but we weren't going to be denied. We wanted to wrestle in that event.

We were still in Nebraska, just a short time after we left Grand Island, when it started snowing.

When we crossed the border into Iowa, it was whiteout conditions. It was not an easy drive. We slowed down and took our time.

HOW GRAND ISLAND BECAME A NEBRASKA WRESTLING DYNASTY

It finally calmed down when we drove into Minnesota.

We were in two 15-passenger school buses with coaches driving. We had 20 wrestlers and a handful of coaches on the trip.

What should have been a nine-hour drive took almost 12 hours. The weather was so bad that Class B Nebraska power Omaha Skutt backed out of The Clash that year.

We wanted to compete at The Clash. We had a team that we thought was good and we knew we had to be tested.

There were some really strong teams from all over the country, and several were nationally ranked.

We made the finals of our eight-team bracket before we wrestled Apple Valley. They were a national powerhouse from just outside the Twin Cities, and they beat us soundly.

Destin McCauley was one of the studs that was wrestling for Apple Valley. Destin was national high school wrestler of the year and was a big recruiting target for NCAA Division I schools.

He started his college career at the DI level before winning a Division II national title for Nebraska-Kearney.

Jake Waste, also on that Apple Valley team, started his college career at the Division I level before he won a DII national title for California Baptist.

Apple Valley was ranked in the top five in the country. They were really good, and we only won four matches against them.

It was a great opportunity for us to measure ourselves against an elite program.

We went 2-1 that first day, and we felt good about how our guys had competed.

We wrestled more good teams the next day and went 1-2. We finished seventh overall. We lost a tough dual to Waverly-Shell Rock, a strong program from Iowa. The Go-Hawks had a number of kids that went on to wrestle at the Division I level in college.

We had beaten nationally recognized Vacaville, California, but lost on the second day to Roseville, Oregon before finishing with a win over Kasson-Mantorville, Minnesota.

We went into The Clash with high expectations. There were some tough teams in there and we discovered first-hand what it was like to measure up against some of the best programs in the coun-

PURPLE REIGN

try. It was a great test.

We wanted to win a couple more of those duals, but it was still a heck of an experience.

We learned we needed to be tougher and we came home with plenty to work on.

The Clash is a great event and I'm so glad we were able to compete in it.

I left feeling fantastic about the event, how our kids competed and what we learned.

It was a very well-run event. They were happy to have us there and they treated us great.

We were honored to be there and felt we performed above expectations at our first national level event.

And we made the national rankings again during the 2009-10 season.

We continued to wrestle well after The Clash.

We went to the Top of the Rockies event in Colorado and we won the 32-team tournament.

The prestigious event is held in Lafayette, Colorado, located just northwest of Denver.

We finished with 178 points and Roosevelt (Colorado) was second with 163.

We won the tournament despite not crowning an individual champion.

We had eight medalists and we put three wrestlers in the finals.

Nate Westerby lost to Connor Medbery of Loveland (Colorado) in the 215-pound finals. Medbery was an excellent wrestler who was nationally ranked. He went on to wrestle for the University of Wisconsin. He was an NCAA runner-up for the Badgers in 2017.

Andrew Riedy also made the finals that year before placing second at 119 pounds.

Our kids battled and did a good job.

It was a tough tournament and a great learning experience for our kids. Our wrestlers had an opportunity to see what it was like to be an elite high school team.

HOW GRAND ISLAND BECAME A NEBRASKA WRESTLING DYNASTY

It was the first time during my tenure at Grand Island that we had wrestled extensively against a number of teams from other states in an individual tournament format.

We had a strong team and we wanted to expose our kids to stronger competition outside of Nebraska.

This helped our kids get out of their comfort zone and also gave them an opportunity to show we could compete against some of the nation's top teams.

Our wrestlers were excited about having some new opportunities to see great competition.

We really strengthened our schedule that season and it paid off.

Winning the Top of the Rockies was really exciting for us. We flexed our muscles a little bit and it showed us we were heading in the right direction. It was a homecoming for me to go back to Colorado, where I had wrestled in college.

There were some very good teams in that tournament, so it was a nice accomplishment for us to win.

Back home, we were very successful wrestling in the state of Nebraska and competing against teams in our conference.

By the time the postseason rolled around, we were ready to go.

We thought we had a chance to break our state tournament scoring record from the year before. We knew it could be done. It wasn't something we talked a lot about, but it was a goal for us.

We were focusing more on everybody's individual performance.

I always coached kids to just ~~worry~~ *Focus* about their own performance and prepare both mentally and physically to compete. Then everything else would take care of itself.

In 2010, sophomore Andrew Riedy won his second state title. He won at 119 pounds. Also earning titles were Blake Fruchtl (125), Carlos Rodriguez (130), Matthew Rice (135) and Nate Westerby (215).

Fruchtl and Westerby also repeated as state champions.

Our wrestlers turned in another dominant performance, outscoring runner-up Kearney 228.5-161.5. We had broken 200

PURPLE REIGN

points for the second straight year.

We crowned five champions, but it wasn't easy. Four of our five wins in the state finals were by a total of six points.

Riedy started our own parade of champions by edging Millard South's Jake Miller by a 2-1 score at 119 pounds.

It was a tight match. Fruchtl had beaten Miller the year before in overtime in the finals by the same score.

Miller was good defensively. Andrew had the lead late in the match and he kept shooting on him.

It was nerve-wracking because he had the lead and he didn't want to give up any points. But Andrew also didn't want to get called for stalling.

Andrew was a gamer and he was confident. He knew what he needed to do and he was going to get it done.

Blake Fruchtl, another sophomore, followed suit by capturing his second state title. He pinned Omaha North's Kenny Martin in the 125-pound finals.

Kenny Martin took Blake down three times and was winning handily. Kenny was up by a handful of points going into the third period.

I had no idea what they were doing, but they put Kenny down to start the third period.

Blake broke Martin down and turned him for a three-point near fall and began to take control of the match. Blake was a hammer on top. He rode a lot of people.

Blake turned him again and he ended up cross-facing him and walking him over before the referee slapped the mat. He had pinned Martin.

I went crazy. I was so pumped. I couldn't believe he pinned him.

It was an incredible comeback.

Blake was being dominated until they put Kenny down. He chose bottom in the third period after being dominant on his feet. It made no sense.

Blake received his opportunity in the third period and he took advantage of it. It was unbelievable that he came back and won.

Sophomore Carlos Rodriguez followed by avenging a loss from the 2009 state finals, reversing the outcome with a 3-2 win over Omaha Central's Tyrell Galloway at 130 pounds.

Carlos had lost a high-scoring match to him the year before.

He came back and redeemed himself.

I remember being extremely excited that we had won that match.

We won three big matches in a row. What a great start to the day.

We could've lost all three of those matches although Andrew and Carlos were in control for the most part.

Blake's win was unexpected.

We made it four straight wins in the finals after Matthew Rice downed Cody Green of Papillion-La Vista South 3-1 in the 135 finals.

Matt didn't have a full arsenal of moves, but he was very good at the moves that he did have.

He was good off the bottom, and he would execute moves like slide-bys and shrugs against anybody.

Cody Green was ranked No. 1 all year and favored to win. Matt had placed fifth and third at state before advancing to the finals as a senior in 2010.

We were in a very tight match and had some scrambles, but nobody scored.

Late in the match, Matt caught Cody leaning and hit him with a slide-by for the winning takedown. He won it in the last seconds.

It was a dramatic win.

I jokingly refer to Matt as one of the luckiest wrestlers because he finished his final three seasons with a win. Not many people can say that. In all seriousness, he did a great job to earn that win in the state finals. He delivered in the clutch.

Matt wasn't a great athlete, and he wasn't overly strong or physical, but he was good enough in certain areas where he could excel.

He was a tough kid with a funky style. He was really flexible and he could make things happen.

PURPLE REIGN

Matt was in a tough practice room and that just made him better. Our room was incredibly tough.

Matt also had the right mindset. He believed he could do it.

That was an upset win for Matt, but it didn't surprise us.

Matt's win had given us four state champions.

We swept state titles at 119, 125, 130 and 135 pounds.

And there was more to come.

Nate Westerby repeated as state champion when he earned a hard-fought 3-1 overtime win over Norfolk's Jordan Heiderman in the 215-pound finals.

We had crowned our fifth state champion.

It was the first time Nate had wrestled Heiderman.

Nate had been banged up that season. He got hurt in a match at The Clash.

After that, Nate came down with mononucleosis and he was out for a month.

He came back for districts, but his conditioning wasn't where it had been.

Nate advanced to face Heiderman in the finals at districts. The tournament was in Norfolk and their fans were really mad when we forfeited in the finals.

The Norfolk fans had an axe to grind with us for some reason. There was some ugliness with that particular situation, but it really didn't matter. I was there to take care of business and more importantly to take care of my kids and my team.

Nate had come back, but he was still sick. He came back earlier than expected because of the timing of the district tournament.

Their match in the state finals was low-scoring.

It was 1-1 going into overtime. Both guys had scored an escape in regulation.

Overtime started and Nate was on the attack. He hit a leg attack and lifted Heiderman to score the winning takedown.

Nate hit a high-crotch, a position and technique we practiced daily, and he executed the finish flawlessly to secure the win and his second title.

It was awesome to see the emotion we all had after he won.

It was a huge release of excitement and energy.

It was great to see Nate end his career as a two-time state champion.

It was understandable why he was so emotional about the win. He fought through not feeling 100 percent to win another state title.

Our sixth finalist, Alan Taylor, reached the championship match for the second straight year. He lost by fall against Matthew Lenagh of Millard North in the 189-pound finals.

Alan was a senior that year. He and Nate trained together and both had a lot of success for us in the heavier weight classes.

Alan was a three-time state medalist and two-time finalist. He had a good career for us and won a lot of big matches. And he was a big part of two state championship teams for Grand Island.

Our list of state medalists in 2010 also included Cameron Mettenbrink (third at 145 pounds), Trey Trujillo (fourth at 103), Cory Frankenberg (fourth at 285), Beau Jepson (fifth at 160) and Coleman Westerby (sixth at 171).

We finished with 11 state medalists in 2010, including six finalists and five champions.

We crowned one more state champion in 2010 than we did in our record-setting season in 2009.

Mettenbrink was a senior on that team and a kid who fought through a lot of adversity to finish his senior year. In his early years, he toiled away in the junior varsity lineup behind several state medalists and champions.

On a couple of occasions, Cameron was in my office telling me he wanted to quit wrestling.

"What's the point," he asked, "if I can't be on varsity?"

On every occasion, I outlined the benefits of sticking with it.

On a state championship team with five champions, Cameron's third-place medal will always be a highlight. I couldn't have been any prouder of him for fighting through everything to not only make the starting lineup his senior year, but to come through with a high medal place for himself and to help our team. He was proud of himself and I was proud of him. Those moments when he decided not to quit helped define his life.

As a coach, it was gratifying to see our team hit its peak again when it counted most. Not many teams have had five state champions in one season.

Athletes work all season, and offseason, with the goal of performing their best when the stakes are highest.

And our wrestlers were able to deliver at the most opportune time.

It was an impressive showing. Being the defending state champion was new and uncharted territory for us.

Especially when they knew we were the favorite and that we were the team that everybody was looking to knock off.

We had a great season.

There were so many things to be proud of and excited about.

A coach always wants to do better. I was looking at all of the could haves and would haves.

We didn't have state champion Alec Chanthapatheth back from the year before.

Alec landed in some trouble off the mat following his junior season and he wasn't with us during his senior year.

It was one of the highest point totals in Class A history.

I was always in search of perfection, so I felt like we could've done a little more. Coaches are always looking at ways to improve and evolve.

And looking at where maybe a team came up short in certain areas.

But it was still a very good year for us. Our program had reached the top in the state and our athletes were determined to stay there.

Initially, I thought we might be able to win two or three state titles as a team. But after we won our first two titles in 2009 and 2010, those expectations changed.

We were very excited to see what the future would hold for us.

With the wrestlers we had returning, we figured we would have an opportunity to contend for state titles in the next two or three years.

We had an experienced group plus we had some other young studs coming up through the ranks.

I couldn't wait for the next season to begin.

The 2009-10 season will always have special meaning for those involved with the Grand Island wrestling program.

We dedicated that season to Mike McClaren, whose son, Tanner, was a member of our wrestling team at Grand Island.

Mike lost his life when he and Tanner were involved in an accident in eastern Colorado. The van he was driving collided with part of a semi that had rolled due to high winds in June 2009.

Tanner McClaren, who was just 15 at the time, suffered minor injuries in the accident.

It was a tragic situation and one that you cannot prepare for.

We came together as a program and community to support Tanner and his family.

We wore purple wristbands that season to honor Mike.

The wristbands had a cross on them with words that read:

"In memory of Mike McClaren – Be the Hammer"

Everybody affiliated with the team wore them. We also had shirts made that we wore that honored Mike.

I had known Mike for a number of years.

He won Class C state titles for Grand Island Central Catholic in 1982 and 1983 at 112 and 119 pounds.

And then he wrestled at Chadron State. He had a good career with them. He was a four-time national qualifier in college and ranks in Chadron State's top 10 in career victories.

Mike student taught at Alliance when I was in middle school in the late 1980s. He taught the woodworking and shop classes that I was in.

When we later reconnected in Grand Island, Mike helped coach many of the kids that we had coming up through the youth ranks.

Mike was a high-energy guy. He was like a little kid on Mountain Dew. He was a smaller guy who would jump on the mat and scrap with the kids. He loved wrestling and he loved staying involved with the sport.

PURPLE REIGN

He was another big piece of the puzzle in helping the Grand Island kids learn and develop.

His son, Tanner, was part of that amazing class with Andrew Riedy, Blake Fruchtl, Carlos Rodriguez and Coleman Westerby.

That was one of the best classes of wrestlers to ever come through Nebraska. They all grew up together and had wrestled together since they were little kids.

We had a pretty close-knit group.

It obviously was a horrible and tragic situation.

It was extraordinarily traumatic for Tanner because he was there when it happened.

That's a lot for a young man to deal with.

Everybody just tried to be there to help and to rally around the family.

Tanner McClaren would go on to place third at state for us at 119 pounds in 2011.

To have Tanner come though and be a state medalist was awesome. Tanner's older brother, Chase, had also been a part of the program and spent time in the varsity lineup.

After his father died, it was difficult for me personally to be as hard on Tanner as I was on some of the other kids.

I wanted him to know he was loved and cared for. To his credit, he fought through a lot of adversity in practice and in his matches to have a good career in wrestling.

I was proud of how he came through to win a medal at the state tournament.

CHAPTER 6
THREE-PEAT

What are the odds of scoring 228.5 points two years in a row at the state wrestling tournament? I'm not sure what they are, but that's exactly what we did.

In 2011, we matched our Class A winning point total from 2010.

And we captured our third straight state championship.

Junior Andrew Riedy (130 pounds) earned his third straight state title while Carlos Rodriguez (140) won his second state title.

Trey Trujillo (112) and Michael Bolan (145) also won state championships for Grand Island that season.

We were still the big dog on the block. We were heavily favored to win state again going into that season and our team was able to deliver with another strong performance.

Our schedule was ridiculously tough, but that's the way we wanted it.

We returned to The Clash and the Top of the Rockies events again for the second straight year.

We were excited to go on those big trips and test ourselves against some extremely strong competition.

We wanted to be better and we wanted to improve. Those rugged events would provide an excellence gauge for us to see where we ranked in comparison to where we wanted to be. And also expose some of our weaknesses we had. It would add new challenges for us in the practice room.

PURPLE REIGN

We wanted to build on what we accomplished in the previous two seasons.

We had a proven and experienced team at almost every weight class, but we did need to find a heavyweight.

Gone was two-time state medalist and heavyweight anchor Cory Frankenberg. The cupboard at heavyweight was essentially bare.

The numbers in our program had started to diminish. In the mid-2000s, we carried 55-60 wrestlers – by 2011 we were lucky to carry 50 kids by Christmas time.

Some couldn't handle the pressure and many kids backed away. It was difficult to keep junior varsity kids happy and motivated to stick around for the prize that waited for them if they were persistent.

The proof was there – kids like Cameron Mettenbrink toiled away and as a senior made the lineup and placed at the state tournament. Ultimately, the machine that we had become rolled on. I hated that I couldn't spend more time with some of those fringe kids, but I felt my focus had to stay on the varsity lineup and keep them on track.

We won our first dual at The Clash over Arrowhead High School, a strong program from Wisconsin.

We went on to drop our next five dual meets, including some close battles where we came up just short.

We still won plenty of individual matches that year, and it was a great experience for our wrestlers.

One funny caveat to The Clash was over the three trips we made to Rochester, every year we matched up with Kasson-Mantorville. Of the three duals over three trips, this year K-M finally got the best of us. Kasson-Mantorville was located in Minnesota and produced such future college stars as the University of Iowa's Sam Stoll and the University of Minnesota's Brady Berge.

We also had a good experience at the Top of the Rockies tournament a few weeks later.

We had won the tournament the year before, but still had a respectable showing in 2011 to place seventh in a very strong 29-

team field.

Pomona, a school in Colorado, won the title with 176.5 points.

We finished just outside the top five with 116.5 points.

By that time, we had lost Blake Fruchtl to disciplinary action for the year. That was a huge hit to our program. We also had other wrestlers who had some issues and were suspended from the Top of the Rockies.

Among the champions that year were Bryce Meredith of Cheyenne Central in Wyoming and Connor Medbery of Loveland High School in Colorado.

Both wrestlers went on to become finalists at the NCAA Division I tournament.

We ended up with two finalists at the Top of the Rockies tournament in 2011.

Trey Trujillo reached the finals for us at 112 pounds.

Trey dropped an 11-9 decision to Darin Sisneros of Alamosa (Colorado) in the championship bout.

Trey was wrestling well and he was on track to achieve his goal of winning a state title that season.

Andrew Riedy was our other finalist at 130 pounds.

Andrew did what he did best. He won a big match.

He earned a 4-3 decision over C.J. York of Roosevelt in the championship bout.

Andrew once again was on track to have a great season and to reach his goal of winning his third straight state championship in 2011. If the pressure was bothering him, we never knew it. He took it all in stride.

Andrew's level of confidence and composure served him well in all of the big matches that he won for Grand Island Senior High. He was such a mature young man for his age.

Wrestling top-flight competition from other states provided us with a significant boost.

And prepared us for our biggest tournaments of the season when we returned to Nebraska.

We had another strong regular season and we entered the postseason with high hopes.

PURPLE REIGN

We arrived at the 2011 state tournament with plenty of momentum.

Andrew Riedy began his quest for a third consecutive state title with a strong first day.

He powered to a pair of wins to start the state tournament before running into a tough opponent in the 130-pound semifinals.

Andrew, as he did so many times in his brilliant career, came through in a big match.

He earned a gritty 4-2 win over Kavon Jones of Omaha North.

Kavon had beaten Andrew earlier in the year at the Creighton Prep Invitational. It was the only in-state loss that Andrew had during his high school career.

In the rematch, Andrew was determined. He was not going to be denied.

He took a 1-0 lead after a penalty point on Jones in the first period.

In the second period, Andrew put Jones on his back for two near-fall points. He had taken a 3-0 lead.

That was more than enough for Andrew to prevail in what was one of the biggest wins of his remarkable career.

Andrew wrestled a sharp match. To get that win over a quality wrestler like Kavon was huge.

Andrew was always a kid that we could strategically set up a game plan for and he could follow it perfectly. It was a mere formality for him to go out and execute it.

Of course, it didn't come without plenty of anxiety from his father and I coaching in the corner. But Andrew's poise was so impressive.

He was so intelligent – one of the smartest wrestlers I ever coached.

He would follow a game plan and do what was necessary to win the match. His level of confidence never seemed to waver. He believed he was going to win. I sat in Andrew's corner for more than 100 matches and I'm not sure I ever saw him fearful. His demeanor and his composure were incredible. Losing wasn't an option when he wrestled at the state tournament.

HOW GRAND ISLAND BECAME A NEBRASKA WRESTLING DYNASTY

With his win over Jones, Andrew had reached the state finals for the third consecutive season.

The state tournament wasn't seeded, so Andrew's toughest match occurred in the semis.

He walked in the Parade of Champions for the third time before wrestling in the finals once again.

He took charge early in the championship bout and quickly eliminated any chances of an upset.

Andrew was in control as he earned an 11-0 major decision over Jacob Oertle of Kearney in the 138-pound finals.

Andrew had won his third state championship.

And he had become the first three-time state champion in Grand Island's storied wrestling history.

He also had positioned himself for a chance to make history the following year.

He would have the opportunity to become a four-time state champion.

Andrew had already been on quite a journey in his first three years of high school.

His first state title was amazing, exciting and unreal – everything you would expect when a freshman wins a state title. It was a great accomplishment.

And then he won his next two state titles and he continued to build momentum.

He had wrestled really well, but it wasn't easy for him.

Andrew had to battle through some very tough challenges in each of those years. He had to win a big match at one point in each of his trips to the state tournament.

He was our leader and he led by example when he stepped on the mat.

We were all excited about having Andrew Riedy back in purple for one more season.

After Andrew won, junior Carlos Rodriguez was up for his third straight finals appearance.

And he followed suit with a big victory at 140 pounds.

Carlos captured his second straight state championship. And

PURPLE REIGN

in impressive fashion.

Carlos controlled Preston Lauterbach of Bellevue West 9-2 in the finals. Lauterbach went on to win a junior-college national championship for Iowa Western Community College before wrestling at Colorado State-Pueblo at the NCAA Division II level.

The win Carlos had over Lauterbach wasn't his biggest win of the tournament.

One of the most anticipated matches of the 2011 state meet came when Carlos battled Tyrell Galloway of Omaha Central in the semifinal round.

Those two had a long history of competing against each other in big matches.

Galloway beat Carlos in the 2009 state finals before Carlos avenged that loss by beating Galloway in the 2010 state championship match.

Their third meeting at state wasn't nearly as close.

Carlos came out aggressively and was on the attack early. There was no doubt who was going to win.

Carlos earned a dominating 10-2 win over Galloway by major decision.

It was an impressive performance. And Carlos was in control the whole way.

He came out strong right away and took command of the bout. Carlos had a unique style and the way he wrestled was the antithesis of Andrew Riedy.

You could wind Carlos up, turn him loose and let him go.

He had unbelievable hips, and he was very powerful.

He would stop people from scoring. He would overpower them and shut them down.

Carlos wrestled a very good wrestler named Jake Sueflohn from Wisconsin at The Clash that year. He ended up losing the match, but Carlos came out and took Jake down and put some points up on him. Sueflohn won the match and went on to wrestle in college for the University of Nebraska. He had a good career for the Huskers.

Wrestling tough kids like Sueflohn was important for us. And those experiences ultimately made us better and it made Carlos better.

Carlos Rodriguez would put on a show when he got out there. His matches were always exciting and entertaining.

It was awesome to see him win his second state title. He had improved every year and his progression was evident at his third state tournament.

Before Andrew and Carlos won their state titles, Trey Trujillo was our first state champion of the day.

Trey earned a 3-2 win over Keygan Foster of Omaha Central in the 112-pound finals.

It was a good, hard-fought win over a tough wrestler.

I coached Trey for a lot of years. That was his best year. He was motivated, driven and focused. He was a little bulldog. He was short, stocky and explosive at 112 pounds.

Trey was an intimidating figure for the typically taller and skinnier kids in that weight class.

He was a 112-pounder who could bench press 250 pounds. He was really strong.

He went out there and bullied people.

He could throw headlocks. He would also shoot high crotches and lift people into the air.

That was definitely Trey's year. And he had the state championship to prove it.

Our final champion that year came at 145 pounds when Mike Bolan defeated Nick Schroeder of Omaha Westside 4-3 in the finals.

Mike was a good athlete and a skilled wrestler. He had the total package.

It was his senior year and he was determined to go out on top.

That was a very big win for Mike and it was a great way for him to cap his career.

He wrestled a great match against his opponent from Omaha Westside. He battled through some tough scrambles in that bout.

It was a back-and-forth, challenging match, but Mike got it done.

PURPLE REIGN

We finished with four state champions in 2011.

That increased our total number of individual state titles to 13 over three seasons.

It was awesome to see so many of our wrestlers be rewarded for their hard work.

We also had two other finalists during that 2010-11 season in Dante Rodriguez (103) and Coleman Westerby (189). They both finished second.

Dante was a talented wrestler with a tremendous upside, but he was small for the 103-pound class. He didn't even weigh 100 pounds that year. We tried to put some weight on him, but he only weighed around 97 pounds for most of the weigh-ins that year.

Dante made up for it by being a good young wrestler.

We were excited about Dante's future with us. The best was yet to come.

Coleman Westerby dropped a hard-fought 8-7 decision to Derek Geddings of South Sioux City in the finals.

That was a tough one. It was a match we felt like we could win and it was a match that easily could've gone the other way. Coleman was a big move guy who pinned a lot of people.

He was powerful, explosive and athletic. He could really dominate his opponents.

That was a crazy match with Geddings. Coleman wrestled a tough kid.

Coleman wrestled a good match, but he couldn't quite close it out. He still had a good season for us and he wrestled well.

We also had state medalists in Tanner McClaren (third at 119 pounds), Billy Leetch (third at 152), Daniel Sotelo (third at 285), Luke McGregor (fifth at 125) and Jeffrey Brisbin (fifth at 171).

It was great to see Tanner perform well less than two years after his father had passed away.

Tanner won by fall in his first match at state before losing by fall in the quarterfinals.

He followed by going on a strong run on the back side of the bracket.

Tanner won four straight matches, including a 5-3 win over

Hayden Hanson of Omaha Creighton Prep.

Hanson went on to win state the next season at 126 pounds.

Tanner capped his remarkable run with a 1-0 win over Asa Stansbury of Kearney in the third-place match.

He won the final four matches of his season.

He really wrestled well and that was great to see. I was proud of him for how he performed. He had a good state tournament.

I can't imagine how difficult that time must have been for him. Wrestling was a sport that really bonded Tanner with his father.

Luke McGregor was a big surprise for us in the postseason that year.

He was a freshman, and had wrestled on the junior varsity most of the season and had been pretty successful.

I had a tough decision to make going into the postseason.

I was considering entering Luke as our 125-pounder at districts. We also had another tough freshman, Andrew Rojas, who we were looking at.

Andrew had wrestled 119 for the JV and Luke had been at 125. Both kids had done well that season wrestling for the junior varsity.

Andrew had beaten Luke in a wrestle-off late in the season for the varsity spot at 125 pounds.

We entered Andrew at the conference tournament, but then Andrew lost to two kids who Luke had beaten earlier in the season.

We were looking at possible seeds for districts and knew that Luke would've been seeded higher than Andrew at districts.

I eventually made the decision to enter Luke for the district tournament instead of Andrew.

It was a very tough call and not one that I enjoyed. I did what I felt was best for the team. I talked to my assistant coaches before I made the final decision.

The move ended up paying off for us.

Luke had a great state tournament, placing fifth in Class A. He scored a lot of points for us.

Andrew Rojas came back strong and had a good career for us.

PURPLE REIGN

If I had a crystal ball, Andrew may have been a better choice since Luke did not finish his high school career in wrestling. However, I stand by our decision and I felt at that time Luke was the better option for that postseason. It was a difficult decision to make – and even worse trying to justify and explain my decision.

In the end, it worked out.

Our winning point total at state of 228.5 points saw us go well over the 200-point plateau for the third straight season.

Kearney was a distant second with 135.5 points.

All 13 of our state qualifiers scored points that year, which was great to see.

We had our share of stars, like Andrew Riedy and Carlos Rodriguez, but we also had plenty of other strong kids who made important contributions as well.

We had a lot of depth and that was evident during those championship seasons. We had so many kids contributing.

That depth meant we had great competition in our practice room. That was important in the development and maturation of our guys.

One of the best stories of that season was our heavyweight, Daniel Sotelo.

Daniel was born in Mexico and moved to the United States when he was in fourth grade.

He was an excellent football player for Grand Island Senior High, and he drew the attention of a number of college recruiters.

I saw that first-hand as an assistant football coach for Grand Island. He was a heck of a player.

Daniel was selected to play in the Shrine Bowl all-star game, and he played college football at the NCAA Division II level for Chadron State.

He was a good-sized high school athlete at 6-foot-3 and 280 pounds. He had the size and strength to be a good wrestler.

During his senior year, we tried to convince him to come out for the sport. We knew we had a glaring hole in our lineup at heavyweight because we knew Daniel could really help us.

We sold Daniel on the fact that wrestling was a sport that

would help his balance, his strength and his endurance for football.

And it did.

Daniel didn't join the Grand Island Senior High wrestling team until after Christmas.

Among our first competitions after he joined the team were our two toughest events of the season – The Clash in Rochester, Minnesota and the Top of the Rockies tournament in Colorado.

He lost a combined six matches in those events, which featured some of the top teams in the country.

We threw Daniel right to the wolves. He took some lumps, but those experiences helped him. He started by wrestling against strong competition and at the level that we would expect any kid in our program to wrestle.

You could tell he hadn't been out there on the mat much. It was a little awkward and uncomfortable for him.

We had a great team, but we didn't have a true heavyweight until Daniel came along.

With such a short window, we decided to just teach him a few basic moves.

We taught him how to stay in good position. We taught him a downblock and a go-behind where he could score off an opponent's shot attempt. And we taught him a collar tie and a slide-by where he could score a takedown by initiating the action.

We wanted Daniel to overpower kids and we gave him a couple simple techniques to be able to do that.

He learned how to stand up and get away. That was important, especially for a heavyweight. He didn't want to get trapped underneath his opponent.

We taught him basic techniques so he could function.

Daniel entered the district tournament at Lincoln Southeast with a 4-12 record.

His record was misleading because he had lost to some really good kids in some very tough events.

But none of that mattered when the postseason started.

He would have the same opportunity as everyone else at the district tournament.

PURPLE REIGN

Coach Dobson gives me instructions during the 1986 kids' freestyle state tournament.

Looking studious after winning the Class A district title for Alliance High School in 1992. Brian Sybrandts of Grand Island was the runner-up. Brian coached Grand Island Northwest to the 2019 Class B state title.

HOW GRAND ISLAND BECAME A NEBRASKA WRESTLING DYNASTY

Looking serious for the cameras at Adams State media day.

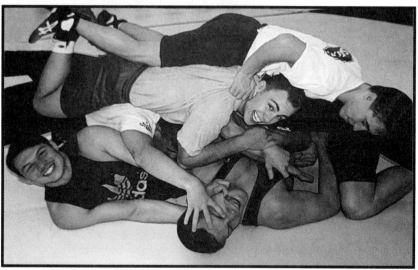

Having some fun goofing around with my Adams State teammates. I'm the goofball in the middle.

PURPLE REIGN

The first college tournament that I won after capturing the 1996 RMAC title as the No. 4 seed.

Having my hand raised after my 1996 win over No. 1 NCAA seed Travis Bonneau of Portland State.

HOW GRAND ISLAND BECAME A NEBRASKA WRESTLING DYNASTY

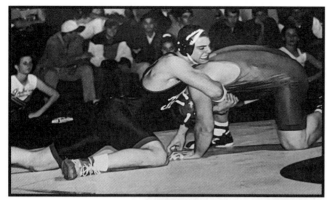

Controlling an opponent with a front headlock during my college days at Adams State.

The referee flies through the air as he is about to slap the mat when Justin Portenier records a fall to win the 2002 NAIA national title.

It was a tremendous honor to coach Justin Portenier, the wrestler I'm congratulating after he won the 2002 NAIA national title for Dakota Wesleyan.

PURPLE REIGN

The cover of the Grand Island newspaper's sports section the day after Brandon Hudiburgh's upset win in the 2006 state finals.

Grand Island team poster for the 2009-10 season.

HOW GRAND ISLAND BECAME A NEBRASKA WRESTLING DYNASTY

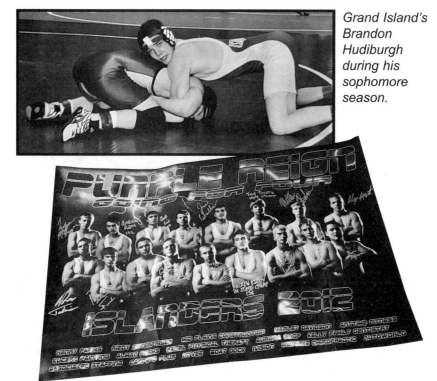

Grand Island's Brandon Hudiburgh during his sophomore season.

The signed Grand Island poster as we prepared to make a run at our fourth straight Class A state title.

Reacting to a big win by GI's Matthew Rice in 2010.

PURPLE REIGN

Grand Island's Andrew Riedy (far right) is shown in 2012 before winning his fourth state title and being on his fourth state championship team. He was joined by these team members. Top, from left: Dante Rodriguez, Ben Najera, Carlos Rodriguez, Jose Ceballos, Austin Leetch and Dorin Hall. Bottom row, from left: Trey Trujillo, John Mottl, Andrew Rojas, Matt Bolan, Billy Thompson and Haris Talundzic.

Riedy tries to take down Omaha Burke's Jared Green.

HOW GRAND ISLAND BECAME A NEBRASKA WRESTLING DYNASTY

Riedy acknowledges the crowd in 2011. It was awesome to be in his corner during his amazing career.

Riedy takes control against Millard North's Devon Rupp during their 138-pound final in Class A. Riedy won 15-0 to capture his fourth state title in 2012.

PURPLE REIGN

Chase Reis celebrates after delivering in Omaha.

Trey Trujillo executes a backflip after capturing a state title.

HOW GRAND ISLAND BECAME A NEBRASKA WRESTLING DYNASTY

Dante Rodriguez looks to finish for a single-leg takedown.

Dante Rodriguez was a bonus-point scoring machine for us.

PURPLE REIGN

Coaching with Zac Dominguez, who runs a highly successful wrestling club in Omaha.

With assistant coach Rob Riedy at the Top of the Rockies event in Colorado.

HOW GRAND ISLAND BECAME A NEBRASKA WRESTLING DYNASTY

Checking out the action during a dual.

Shouting instructions from the bench with assistant coach Rob Riedy.

Austin Leetch locks a spladle up on an opponent from Apple Valley.

PURPLE REIGN

Carlos Rodriguez had a heck of a career for us, winning two state titles and reaching the state finals all four years.

Blake Fruchtl did a tremendous job for GISH, capturing state titles as a freshman and sophomore.

Celebrating our first Class A state team title in 2009.

Billy Leetch looks for a fall.

Matt Rice looks to turn an opponent.

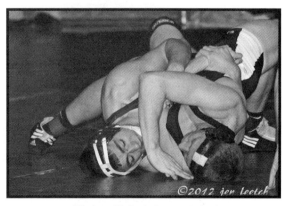

Chase Reis takes control.

PURPLE REIGN

Grand Island's 2011 state championship team.

Billy Leetch looks to lock up a cradle.

Matt Rice gains the upper hand in a match.

HOW GRAND ISLAND BECAME A NEBRASKA WRESTLING DYNASTY

Austin Leetch dominates an opponent.

Jeff Westerby was another coach who made great contributions to the G.I. program.

Joined by past Grand Island head coaches Rod Shada and Kurt Frohling. We combined for nearly 50 years of running the Islander wrestling program.

PURPLE REIGN

In the corner shouting encouragement to our wrestlers.

Checking out the action during our run of five straight state titles.

Sharing a few words with Dante Rodriguez.

With four-time state champion Andrew Riedy during his induction into the Grand Island Senior High Hall of Fame. Andrew was the model student-athlete who led the way on four state championships teams.

PURPLE REIGN

Our collection of five Class A state championship trophies from 2009-13.

Talking with Zac Dominguez during a book signing at DJ's Dugout between sessions of the 2019 Nebraska state wrestling tournament.

Returning to the level where I started my career as a head coach when I took over at Hastings College in 2014.

HOW GRAND ISLAND BECAME A NEBRASKA WRESTLING DYNASTY

Daniel won his first match at districts by decision over a future state champion from Millard South and followed with a pin to reach the finals.

He then delivered to outlast Lincoln Southeast's Daniel Washington in overtime to capture the district title.

It was awesome. We were going crazy.

Washington was a good athlete and a good football player. And with the win, Daniel qualified for state in wrestling.

That was a huge win and a huge moment for us in a season filled with magical moments.

Daniel entered the state tournament as a district champion, meaning he would meet a fourth-place finisher from another district in the first round.

But Daniel was still a first-year wrestler with little experience. And he was competing in his first state tournament before thousands of fans in a massive arena in Omaha.

Daniel suffered a first-round loss at state, falling 3-1 to Tanner Paxton of Lincoln North Star.

Paxton had beaten Daniel in the conference tournament a couple of weeks before. Paxton moved pretty well and he was a tough matchup for Daniel.

After Paxton beat Daniel at state, Paxton lost his next two matches and fell short of placing.

Daniel stuck around for a little bit longer.

He calmed down and regrouped before going on an amazing and improbable run on the back side of the 285-pound bracket.

Daniel started his march through the wrestlebacks with pins over Ralston's Brian Farley and North Platte's Bradan Erdman.

He followed by defeating Hunter Greer of Omaha Burke 4-2 in overtime to clinch a spot on the medal podium.

But Daniel wasn't done yet. He won his next match by default before running into a familiar foe in the match for third place.

Daniel was matched up against Lincoln Southeast's Daniel Washington, the wrestler he had beaten in overtime the week before in the district finals.

The rematch went into overtime again, and Daniel Sotelo pre-

PURPLE REIGN

vailed again. He defeated Washington 3-2 to secure a third-place finish at state.

It was amazing what Daniel accomplished. He was an average wrestler who lacked experience. But he had so much potential with his physical skills and the tenacity he had shown in football.

When the postseason started, it all started to click for him.

We had been trying to get Daniel to come out for wrestling for quite some time. It was a long process.

Daniel was talented. He was powerful and athletic for his size. We knew he could help our program if we could get him out.

I don't know that we could have predicted that he would place third in the state and win a district title, but nonetheless it happened.

It was incredible what he did. That's one of the enjoyable parts of coaching for me. When young men achieve something that nobody believes is possible.

That's what Daniel Sotelo did.

He was 4-12 entering districts and went 8-1 in the postseason to finish third in the state in Class A.

Daniel said after the state tournament that he wished he would have come out for wrestling as a freshman instead of joining the team as a senior.

I wish that would've happened as well, but it was awesome what he did during the one season he did compete for us.

Daniel's performance was another highlight in a season filled with them.

It was one of the most heartwarming stories I have from those years at Grand Island.

What a huge story it was.

Our kids did an outstanding job during the 2010-11 season, but I still wonder if this team could have broken the state tournament scoring record that we set in 2009.

Blake Fruchtl would've been a junior on our third state championship team. He started the 2010-11 season as a member of our team.

Blake had done a great job for us, winning state titles as a freshman and sophomore in 2009 and 2010.

HOW GRAND ISLAND BECAME A NEBRASKA WRESTLING DYNASTY

Blake had wrestled for us during the first semester of his junior year at 135 pounds. He was undefeated and tearing through everybody.

He looked like was going to roll through the season and win his third state title.

But Blake had some issues off the mat. He had missed some workouts and we knew something was wrong.

He was dealing with some problems away from wrestling. It was a difficult situation.

He was suspended for one year from all school activities at Grand Island Senior High.

He could have come back and wrestled for us after Christmas his senior year. We were optimistic he would come back, but it didn't happen.

Blake instead transferred to Grand Island Northwest for his senior year.

It came as no surprise to me when he won the Class B state title at 145 pounds for Northwest in 2012.

He rolled through his bracket that year at state, recording two pins and a 6-0 victory to reach the state championship for the third time in high school.

Blake then capped his prep career by pinning senior Keith Jadlowski of Omaha Skutt Catholic in the Class B championship match at 145.

He had won his third state title – two for Grand Island and one for Northwest.

It was tough watching Blake wrestle for another team after he had been with us at Grand Island for so long.

I loved coaching Blake, and I really enjoyed being around him.

Blake was such a likeable, dynamic kid who would talk to everybody. He could function in any environment. He just had a magnetic personality and people liked being around him.

During his senior season, I made it a point to find time to watch him wrestle at state.

I watched his state finals match and he hit a big move to win

PURPLE REIGN

his third state title.

I was happy for Blake.

He was on track to be a four-time state champion. I have no doubt in my mind he would've won four state titles if he would have stayed out of trouble.

I believe Blake had talent commensurate with many top NCAA Division II wrestlers at the time and he could have even wrestled at the Division I level in college. He was that good.

Blake Fruchtl finished his high school career by winning championships in all three years he competed in the Nebraska state tournament. He was a combined 12-0 in three trips to Omaha.

Blake was an excellent wrestler who went on to excel at Hastings College.

Blake earned NAIA All-American honors for Hastings in 2014. He advanced to the national semifinals before placing fifth in the country at 141 pounds. He was 38-8 that season.

There was never any question about his abilities as a wrestler. He was an excellent wrestler with a strong skill set. And there was never a question about him competing at a high level when the stakes were highest.

He won more than his share of big matches in his career.

I again became Blake's coach when I took over as the head coach at Hastings College prior to the 2014-15 season.

I tried to keep him on track – I really cared about him and I really wanted him to excel.

Unfortunately, he continued to have issues off the mat and he was eventually dismissed from the team.

It was very tough to have that happen, but I believe Blake is on a good path now. He's such a personable young man who could do so many good things with his life.

CHAPTER 7
BACK 4 MORE

Our superstar class at Grand Island Senior High was finally seniors. It wasn't the way we envisioned it unfolding, but we had won three straight Class A state championships and were favored to win it again in 2012.

Senior standout Andrew Riedy was looking to become the first Grand Island wrestler and the 19th in Nebraska wrestling history to win four state titles.

Carlos Rodriguez would be shooting for his third straight state title.

And young stud Dante Rodriguez was primed to win his first state title after a runner-up finish as an undersized freshman.

We were feeling pretty good about the wrestlers we had in our lineup. We knew we had a very good team returning.

But it was still a battle for us to stay focused.

We had to remember that nothing was given to us. We still had to work hard and train hard. We had to earn it again.

I had to make sure our kids stayed grounded and humbled so they would remain focused and not lose sight of what we were trying to accomplish.

Omaha Burke had a very good team. And we also knew that Omaha North and Millard South were gaining ground.

Those teams were working hard to try and knock us off, just like we were when Millard South was the top dog in Class A.

We had to do more to make sure we could stay ahead of those teams.

We made some changes in our schedule and added more out-

PURPLE REIGN

of-state competitions.

One change came because of the weather.

The opening weekend of competition, there was a snowstorm in the forecast and the Kearney Invitational, an opening weekend staple for the Islanders for decades, was postponed. The event would be rescheduled over the Christmas holiday and we were already scheduled to attend the Creighton Prep Invitational during that time.

I didn't want to be without a tournament that first weekend, so I immediately messaged Cozad coach Derek Hammerlun.

Cozad hosted one of the toughest opening weekend tournaments of the year filled with an outstanding field of Class B schools from all over the state. Coach Hammerlun was welcoming to us and we graciously accepted the opportunity to compete in their tournament.

The storm turned out to be relatively mild and fortunately we didn't have to miss out on competing that first weekend.

We also competed in and hosted a massive two-day, 32-team event that included top-ranked teams from Nebraska, Kansas, Wyoming and Montana.

It would eventually be recognized as the state's premier regular-season event.

When we launched the event in 2007, Grand Island athletic director Joe Kutlas and I were trying to come up with a name for it.

I came up with Flatwater. And Joe, being a former English teacher, offered Fracas.

And the rest is history.

The Flatwater Fracas became the biggest wrestling tournament in the state outside of February's three-day state tournament in Omaha.

The Fracas was held at the Heartland Events Center on the Nebraska State Fairgrounds in Grand Island. The competition was held on 10 mats with a dual-meet format.

Among the top Nebraska teams competing in the Flatwater Fracas were Kearney, Columbus, Omaha Burke and Lincoln East.

We wanted to expand into a bigger tournament than the old

HOW GRAND ISLAND BECAME A NEBRASKA WRESTLING DYNASTY

Grand Island Invitational, a good event with 12 teams.

The Heartland Events Center was being built and I approached our athletic director with the idea of having a monster tournament there.

We started talking about the format.

Did we want to have a tournament with individual champions crowned in each weight class? Or did we want more of a team format with a dual-meet tournament?

Nobody in Nebraska or in that part of the country had a big dual tournament, so that's what we decided to do.

Joe Kutlas and I built the Flatwater Fracas from scratch. And it was a labor of love.

We called around and invited some of the best teams in Nebraska in all four classes to commit to our new event. Then we started contacting teams outside Nebraska. We brought in teams from Cheyenne, Wyoming and Manhattan, Kansas and Billings, Montana.

We had a dozen schools the first year of the Flatwater Fracas and then 24 the next year. The Fracas eventually grew to 32 teams. It continues to be an awesome event.

Kearney and Manhattan won the Fracas the first two years and then we won the next six.

We worked hard to make it a prestigious event. We gave gifts to the head coaches. We sold shirts and tried to make it a very good, fan-friendly event.

We wanted it to be a first-class event and I think we accomplished that.

My vision and my dream for the Fracas was to make it like The Clash in Minnesota.

It was always about finding the best teams and the best officials.

I wanted to include all four classes of Nebraska wrestling schools.

It was one of the best things we did when I was at Grand Island. And it was very well-received.

We had really great support in the community. We had a lot of

PURPLE REIGN

advertisers and sponsors.

The *Grand Island Independent* newspaper did a great job covering the event and including all of the results.

Sportswriter Marc Zavala of the Independent did an awesome job. Marc was the last one in the arena at the end of the day, typing in the results and writing stories. He provided us with a lot of good coverage during those state championship years.

We also would recognize and honor our alumni at the Fracas.

Al Hayman also helped make the Flatwater Fracas a top-notch event. Al was our head night custodian at Grand Island. Al and his crew would clean the mats after the first day of the Fracas. They did a great job, and when we came back for the second day everything looked as good as it did on the first day.

Al's twin sons, Logan and Tanner, wrestled for us. Al was one of the best supporters and biggest fans of the Grand Island program. Logan was a state runner-up and three-time medalist for us. Tanner was a good wrestler who qualified for state.

Logan was a tough, hard-nosed wrestler. Tanner's style was funky and athletic.

The Hayman twins were important to our program when I came to Grand Island. They could be more than a little ornery. They had a lot of extra energy.

We wrestled another great schedule during the 2011-12 season, but we didn't go to one of our favorite events that year.

We missed out on The Clash in Rochester, Minnesota because the dates were changed for the event. We had five days off for the holidays and we were only going to have one day of practice before we went up there.

And there was an issue with the two-pound weight allowance that would've affected us as well.

We liked The Clash. It was a tough competition that tested and challenged us. It was a great event that was very well run. They treated us great up there. But with the schedule change, it just didn't work out for us to compete that season.

Even without The Clash, we still find plenty of ways to test our wrestlers.

HOW GRAND ISLAND BECAME A NEBRASKA WRESTLING DYNASTY

I had been trying to figure out a way to set up a dual meet with Class B state powerhouse Omaha Skutt Catholic.

The SkyHawks were the gold standard in Class B, having won a record 13 consecutive state championships. They also had a number of wrestlers who had excelled on the national level. They were the premier program in the state, regardless of classification.

We were able to schedule a dual, and I was pumped because we would finally have a chance to face them.

We wrestled the much-anticipated dual meet against Skutt Catholic shortly after Christmas.

The SkyHawks also had competed in The Clash and had wrestled in a number of out-of-state competitions as they built their program.

Skutt has gone on to win an all-class state record 20 state titles.

We finally stepped on the mat to face Omaha Skutt Catholic on January 5, 2012 in Lincoln with our dual meet being held prior to the Nebraska-Ohio State college dual.

It was a great opportunity for us to wrestle on the University of Nebraska campus.

And it was a rare matchup between the state's top two wrestling programs at that time. Skutt held the all-class and Class B records for most points in a state tournament. We held the scoring record in Class A.

Both teams were ranked No. 1 in their respective classes and our kids were excited for an opportunity to face them.

It was a good atmosphere to compete in against a top-flight program that we had great respect for.

Coach Brad Hildebrandt had done an amazing job at Skutt Catholic. He led his program to a Class B record 17th state championship before he retired as the school's head coach in 2015.

It was awesome to wrestle against Skutt that night in a college venue. It was a great thing for our kids and a great thing for the sport in Nebraska. It was a great opportunity to showcase that and do it in a great environment.

The dual was entertaining for the fans to watch. There was

PURPLE REIGN

plenty of action and plenty of high-level wrestling.

We took control right away.

Top-ranked Carlos Rodriguez delivered a big win for us in a pivotal matchup early in the meet.

Carlos battled back from a second-period deficit to beat Class B No. 2 Zane Sackett 10-5 at 152 pounds.

Sackett was a state runner-up for Skutt who came from an excellent wrestling family. His brother, Tyler, was a four-time state champion for the SkyHawks.

The win by Carlos gave us a 6-0 lead after the first two matches.

After Skutt standout Grant Randall won at 160 pounds, we were able to rattle off three straight wins to take control.

Adam Talundzic came up huge to score a fall over Nick Jensen at 195, giving us a commanding 18-3 lead.

Skutt battled back when top-ranked J.T. Sloboth recorded a pin early in the second period at 113 pounds. That drew the SkyHawks within 25-15 in the dual.

Three-time state champion Thomas Gilman of Skutt later won by fall at 132 pounds, but we had already clinched the victory. Gilman was a superstar who was ranked No. 1 nationally. He was a Cadet and Junior Nationals champion who had already committed to the University of Iowa.

We had a pretty good three-time state champion of our own in top-ranked Andrew Riedy and he put on a show in the final match.

Andrew put an exclamation point on the victory when he earned a quick and decisive win. He recorded a 15-0 technical fall in the first period at 138 pounds.

Nobody in the state could put points on the scoreboard as quickly as Andrew. He could take a wrestler down, start tilting them to their back and the next thing you know the match was over.

Not many kids could tech someone in the first period, but it was something Andrew did a lot.

It was an enjoyable way to end the night and the dual meet provided us with a great opportunity to measure ourselves against an elite program like Skutt Catholic.

HOW GRAND ISLAND BECAME A NEBRASKA WRESTLING DYNASTY

We earned a 39-21 victory over Skutt before a crowd of 1,200 fans at the NU Coliseum.

It was really huge for us to gain exposure by wrestling before the Husker dual.

We won a lot of the close matches in the dual and that was the difference for us.

We were a pretty seasoned team at that point and had received some national attention.

We had wrestled more than our share of tough competition, so we weren't intimidated to wrestle a powerhouse program like Skutt.

We knew what kind of weight that meet carried for us.

It had been a while since Skutt had lost an in-state dual to anybody in Nebraska.

The meet was a big deal for us. Skutt had been the best team in Nebraska, regardless of class, for a number of years.

It wasn't Brad's best team and it wasn't our best team. But both teams were still strong. The quality of wrestling that night was at a high level.

Our guys also were able to wrestle well again when we left the state during the 2011-12 season. We went back to the Top of the Rockies tournament again in Colorado and our guys did an outstanding job.

And we won the team title again.

We scored 201 points to roll to the tournament championship by 57 points over runner-up Thompson Valley, a strong team from Colorado.

At that point in the season, we were grinding through a very rough part of our schedule in January.

To go out of state and win the Top of the Rockies again, that gave us a huge boost going back to Nebraska for our conference, district and state tournaments.

Our kids were starting to hit their peak.

Sophomore Dante Rodriguez won the 106-pound title at the Top of the Rockies event. He pinned Drew Romero of Bloomfield in the finals.

PURPLE REIGN

He headlocked his opponent to win in dramatic fashion.

Dante was on course to reach his goal of winning his first state title.

Chase Reis finished second in Colorado for us at 170 pounds. He dropped a 5-0 decision to Austin Trujillo of Valley in the finals.

Andrew Riedy finished third at 138 pounds after losing a hard-fought bout in the semifinals. It was a close match that he easily could have won. Andrew was hard to score on – he was very good defensively. He showed a lot of maturity and resolve by coming back to place third in Colorado.

In typical Andrew Riedy fashion, he rolled past Josh Donkle of Windsor by a 15-0 technical fall in the third-place match.

Andrew was consistently good for us. You could always count on him to perform at a high level. He had dropped a match, but he had immediately put it behind him and was dominant in his next bout.

Our heavyweight, Dorin Hall, placed fourth.

We also had fifth-place finishers in Matt Bolan (120), Trey Trujillo (126), Carlos Rodriguez (152) and Billy Thompson (160).

Bolan won by major decision in his fifth-place bout with Trujillo winning by fall and Rodriguez and Thompson winning by decision.

It was fitting that Dante Rodriguez earned a championship for us at the Top of the Rockies tournament.

Dante was a hammer for us that season. He didn't lose a lot of matches in his career.

He was an excellent athlete who was a very good, very dynamic wrestler. He had a huge arsenal of moves and could score in a variety of ways.

He could shoot leg attacks to either side. If somebody wanted to go upper body, he could do that. He had a strong Greco-Roman background and was able to lock up with anybody.

He also had a Twister, a move that was a Kearney staple where a wrestler could turn an opponent to their back out of a front headlock.

Dante grew up in Kearney. He was a good young wrestler, but

he had a dilemma right before he was about to go into his freshman year of high school.

He also was fully aware that if he went to Kearney High School, he likely was going to be sitting the bench behind state champion Hunter Bamford at 106 pounds.

And Dante was too good to be wrestling on the junior varsity. For anybody.

When Dante was in eighth grade, he was legally able to go to school anywhere he wanted. He came to Grand Island Senior High on a visit with his parents, and he liked what he saw.

He chose GISH.

Grand Island is a 40-mile drive east from Kearney on Interstate 80.

Dante wrestled three seasons for us before going back to Kearney High for his senior year.

Dante had an excellent freshman year despite being undersized at the lightest weight class. He placed second in the state for Grand Island behind Hunter Bamford his freshman year.

He made a smart move by leaving Kearney.

He was better than every other 106-pounder in the state. He just couldn't beat the starter at Kearney High.

Dante came back strong as a sophomore and he entered his second state tournament in 2012 on a mission to capture his first championship.

He won by fall in the first period in his first two matches.

He then ran into a tough opponent in the 106-pound semifinals in freshman Nolan Laux of Hastings.

The match was tied 4-4 in regulation before Dante earned a 6-4 win in overtime.

I knew Nolan was a tough kid. His dad was the coach at Hastings High. He was a good scrapper. He was a long, lanky kid who was a lot bigger than Dante. It was a tough matchup.

Nolan went on to win two state titles.

He was a good rider. Dante was still a little undersized at that time.

Dante was able to come through in overtime and score to pull

PURPLE REIGN

out a tough win over Nolan.

I recruited Nolan a few years later when I returned to college coaching, and he wrestled for me at Hastings College.

Nolan qualified for nationals one year for me at Hastings, but he had some shoulder issues.

With the state tournament not seeded, Dante's toughest match in 2012 ended up being his semifinal win over Nolan Laux.

Dante recorded his third pin of the tournament in the finals. He pinned Omaha Burke's Brent Curtis late in the third period of their 106-pound finals bout.

Brent Curtis was a tough wrestler who went on to wrestle in college at Morningside. He was a short, stocky kid who was athletic and could move well.

That was a big win for Dante. He had won his first state championship to cap a great season.

When Dante put kids on their back, it was over. There was no getting out. He was a dangerous wrestler who was always a threat to pin his opponent.

The win by Dante provided a great boost for us. He went right out and won a championship right away.

Andrew Riedy entered his final state tournament as the overwhelming favorite to win his fourth state championship.

But that didn't mean it was a foregone conclusion.

We felt confident in his chances and Andrew was a confident kid who had shown great composure in the biggest matches of the season.

It was kind of business as usual with Andrew going into state. That was how he approached it and obviously what he was doing was working.

He knew what he needed to do.

There was a lot of focus and attention, especially by the media, with Andrew going for his fourth state title.

Two other Nebraska wrestlers were also chasing history that season.

Skutt Catholic's Thomas Gilman was also going for his fourth state title in Class B at 132 pounds.

HOW GRAND ISLAND BECAME A NEBRASKA WRESTLING DYNASTY

Eric Coufal of Howells was looking for his fourth crown in Class D at 132 pounds.

Gilman and Coufal both went on to become NCAA Division I starters at Big Ten schools.

Gilman was a three-time All-American for the University of Iowa who went on to win a world silver medal in freestyle wrestling for the U.S. Coufal went on to become a starter at the University of Nebraska.

There certainly was plenty of attention on the three wrestlers going for their fourth state titles in 2012.

The publicity was good for the sport and it was great for those wrestlers to gain the recognition that they had earned.

But there also was a fair amount of pressure on each of those guys.

I thought Andrew Riedy did a great job at handling the media attention.

He had so much poise. He had everything together and he had a game plan.

Andrew was the type of kid I didn't have to push or drive that much because he was always working hard and doing the right things.

Andrew was a leader in a lot of ways. During our conditioning runs, he would be in front of everybody. He was a workhorse.

He set the tone for us in the way he trained, competed and carried himself.

Andrew was a great leader by example.

When something needed to be said, he wasn't afraid to say it.

He would say something to his teammates if they weren't working hard or needed a little bit of a push.

He certainly modeled the way for us.

Andrew opened his final state tournament by pinning Lane Edwards of Papillion-La Vista South in the second period at 138 pounds.

He followed by earning an 11-0 major decision over Papillion-La Vista's Jimi Wall.

He was halfway to his fourth title.

PURPLE REIGN

Andrew had advanced to the semifinals against a good young wrestler in Omaha Burke sophomore Jared Green.

Andrew battled a strong opponent and emerged with a 4-1 win.

Jared was an athletic kid. That semifinal bout was essentially the finals. It was a good win for Andrew. He wrestled smart and controlled the match.

There weren't a lot of points scored, but Andrew took care of business.

He showed the great composure that made him so successful for us.

Andrew had reached his fourth consecutive state championship match.

He was one win away from becoming Grand Island's first four-time state champion.

Riedy's opponent in his final high school match would be surprise finalist Devon Rupp of Millard North.

I didn't have to give Andrew a motivational speech before his fourth and final state championship match. He was ready. It was a mere formality for him.

I pulled him aside before the finals match and delivered a simple message.

"Go take care of business, bud, you got this."

Andrew simply nodded his head. He was confident and ready to roll.

Rupp had placed fourth at districts and had 10 losses that season, but that didn't matter once he stepped onto the mat at the state tournament.

Rupp won his first two matches by fall before edging Norfolk's Blake Andersen 3-2 in the semifinals.

Rupp had knocked off two district champions en route to the state finals.

Rupp's run of knocking off district champions came to a screeching halt when he stepped onto the mat for the 138-pound finals.

Andrew entered his last match for Grand Island with a 15-0

record in the state tournament, including 3-0 in the finals.

He took control early and rolled to a 15-0 technical fall.

It was a quick match and it was a fitting way for him to cap his high school career with a dominating performance.

The Century Link Center crowd of 12,000-plus fans stood and rewarded Andrew with a standing ovation as an announcement went out in the arena:

"Congratulations to Grand Island's Andrew Riedy. He's a four-time state champion in Class A."

His father, Rob, was in the corner coaching with me.

Rob was emotional and I understand why. It was an amazing father-son moment for the Riedys. They had worked well together over the past four years to achieve this lofty goal.

As Andrew's final high school match ended, Rob Riedy turned and hugged me in the corner. We had sat together coaching in the corner during Andrew's magical four-year run. It was special.

It was very business-like, but it was still an amazing moment.

Winning four state titles against the state's biggest schools in Class A was an impressive feat.

Andrew didn't show a ton of emotion when he won, raising his arms and pointing to the crowd.

I'm sure it was a big relief for Andrew to finish his journey and become a four-time state champion.

After Andrew's hand was raised by the official, he walked over and shook hands with the Millard North coaches.

He then came over and shared a hug with his father and then with me.

And I'm sure he felt a big weight had been lifted off his shoulders.

He didn't show any signs that the pressure bothered him.

The expectations were high for Andrew because of the high level of success he had achieved.

That was a credit to him.

We always put the team first, but it was awesome to be part of a different kind of history that day.

Andrew had won Nebraska Class A state titles at 103, 119,

PURPLE REIGN

130 and 138 pounds from 2009-12.

Andrew was dominant right from the get-go when he started wrestling at the high-school level. We knew he had a chance to be pretty special. He was an incredibly disciplined and skilled wrestler.

Andrew was tough and gritty, and very good technically.

He set Grand Island career records for most wins (169), falls (110) and team points (1,116).

Andrew Riedy is the only wrestler in school history who has won more than two state championships for the Islanders.

"Competing as a member of the state championship team the last four years at Grand Island, the team aspect is so important and makes it so much fun," Riedy said after winning his fourth state title. "I'm proud to be the leader of the best team in the state the last four years."

Andrew also was an excellent student. He was valedictorian at Grand Island Senior High in 2012, ranking No. 1 in his class of 402 students.

"There will be a day when wrestling is over," Riedy said at the state meet in 2012, "but I love it and I love every second of it, from practice to the state tournament."

There are a lot of things that can go wrong when you're trying to become a four-time state champion. But Andrew prevented those from happening.

I was honored and blessed to have an opportunity to coach him.

He won the 2012 Guy Mytty Wrestler of the Year Award in Class A. He went on to wrestle for the University of Nebraska at Kearney, where he earned numerous academic honors as a student-athlete.

Our Grand Island team did a good job keeping everything in perspective as Andrew chased history during the 2011-12 season.

It wasn't about Andrew earning his fourth title. It was more about winning it as a team. We never made it about him.

We also knew we were going to be in a tight team race and we knew we were going to have some challenges.

HOW GRAND ISLAND BECAME A NEBRASKA WRESTLING DYNASTY

We knew the team score would be closer than it had been the previous three years.

We didn't have as much firepower in 2012, but the kids that did place all finished in the top four.

That was huge for us.

It was always about the team first.

It was never about any one, two or three individuals. It was about every single kid, varsity and junior varsity, that was on our team. Every one of those kids played an important role for us. And that was a formula that worked great for us.

Carlos Rodriguez's quest to win a third state title came up short as he ran into an outstanding opponent in the finals.

Carlos started off strong in his final state tournament at 152 pounds.

He recorded two falls and a 10-3 decision to advance to the state championship match for the fourth time in his brilliant career.

Carlos would face a very tough challenge in the finals against Omaha North sophomore and returning state champion JaVaughn Perkins.

Carlos had lost to Perkins, a talented, athletic and skilled wrestler, in the district finals.

Perkins was the youngest of three standout wrestling brothers who combined to win 10 Nebraska state titles.

Carlos dropped a 9-2 decision to Perkins in the final match of his prep career.

Perkins was a dynamic wrestler – he was a phenom. He was one of the best wrestlers in the state. He was a special wrestler and one of the best to ever come out of Nebraska.

JaVaughn Perkins went on to win four state titles before placing second at the NCAA Division II tournament for Colorado State-Pueblo.

Carlos had a great career for us. We couldn't have asked for much more from him during his four years on the varsity.

He was a true success story.

He came from a rough background and had to overcome so many obstacles. He experienced his share of struggles off the mat,

PURPLE REIGN

but he was a consistently strong performer for us.

Wrestling was a sport that gave him direction and had a positive impact on Carlos.

He made the state finals four straight years as an individual and helping us win four state team titles.

When he was a freshman, I never would have believed he would have been a four-time state finalist.

He greatly surpassed the expectations that we had for him. That's a credit to Carlos and his approach to the sport.

He was mentally tough. He was a gamer and he won more than his share of big matches in his career for Grand Island Senior High.

Returning state champion Trey Trujillo advanced to his second straight championship match before placing second for us in 2012 at 126 pounds.

Trey rolled into the finals during his junior season with two pins and a major decision.

He then dropped a 4-3 decision to Omaha Creighton Prep's Hayden Hanson, who had finished third in our district.

That was a tough loss for Trey. He didn't wrestle his best match that day. We all believed he was going to win that match.

Trey was a talented wrestler and we knew he had more good wrestling left in him.

We fully expected him to come back motivated to win state again as a senior.

Grand Island sophomore Chase Reis also made it to the finals before finishing second in the state tournament at 170 pounds.

Chase won by technical fall, fall and major decision in his first three matches before falling to Chris Luehring of Bellevue West by a tech fall in the state championship match.

Luehring went on to wrestle in college at Nebraska-Kearney.

Chase was a sophomore wrestling at 170, so he would be back for two more seasons.

Chase was special to me.

He was a wonderful young man. He was a great leader by example. He would always help other people and he was great with

HOW GRAND ISLAND BECAME A NEBRASKA WRESTLING DYNASTY

kids.

Chase went on to do well in athletics after high school. He was an All-American in football for a Morningside College team that was ranked No. 1 nationally at the NAIA level. He was a starting linebacker for us at Grand Island. He played on the defensive line in college and was a force after growing to 6-foot-2 and 250 pounds.

Chase is a fabulous human being. I think the world of him.

He is a kind, honest, decent kid with a great work ethic.

He is a hard kid not to love. And a hard kid not to root for.

Junior Matt Bolan finished strong to place third at 120. He earned a 4-2 overtime win over Brandyn Burget of Bellevue East to place third. He had beaten Burget 6-1 earlier in the tournament in the quarterfinals.

Andrew Rojas bounced back to have a superb sophomore season before placing fourth at state at 132 pounds.

Senior Austin Leetch added a fourth-place finish for us at 145 pounds.

We finished with eight state medalists, who each finished in the top four in their respective weight classes.

And we had captured our fourth straight Class A team title.

We finished under 200 points for the first time during our historic run of consecutive titles.

But we still managed to score 184 points, 39 more than runner-up Omaha Burke.

Our kids wrestled well and hit their peak again at the most important part of the season.

So many good things were happening, but we also had our share of issues off the mat.

We never reached our full potential as a team.

It's difficult to feel too bad when you've won four consecutive state championships, but we were in a position to do something even more special that season.

Blake Fruchtl would have been a senior on that 2012 Grand Island team. He won state titles for us as a freshman and sophomore before being suspended from the team his junior year.

He came back to win a Class B state title after transferring to

PURPLE REIGN

Grand Island Northwest for his senior season.

I was happy to see Blake finish his prep career with another state title. I loved being around him and loved coaching him. I wanted nothing but the best for Blake.

We also lost Coleman Westerby because of an off-the-mat issue that season. Coleman had been a state runner-up the year before.

Tanner McClaren also was a senior that year, but he elected not to come out for wrestling. He had done a great job for us, placing third at the state tournament in 2011.

Tanner was part of that elite class that included Andrew Riedy, Carlos Rodriguez, Blake Fruchtl and Coleman Westerby.

Tanner was still coping with the tragic loss of his father and it was difficult for a lot of us to imagine just how difficult that period of his life was for him.

Tanner was a great kid who I enjoyed having in our wrestling program.

We suffered huge losses with Andrew Riedy and Carlos Rodriguez finishing their prep careers in 2012.

Andrew and Carlos combined for eight appearances in the state finals and six championships.

They made huge contributions to our program and led us to four straight state team titles.

They would be missed.

Andrew and Carlos had wrestled their last matches for Grand Island Senior High, but we still had plenty of top wrestlers returning.

And we were anxious to make a run at trying to capture a fifth consecutive state championship in Class A.

CHAPTER 8
DRIVE FOR FIVE

Four-time state champion Andrew Riedy had exhausted his eligibility as had four-time state finalist Carlos Rodriguez. Our superstar class that had led Grand Island Senior High to four straight Class A state team championships had graduated.

But we still had a lot of talent coming back and we weren't done.

Even with the departure of Andrew and Carlos, we knew we still had the firepower to make a run at our fifth consecutive state title in 2013.

I knew the margin for error was becoming less and less.

We still had a group of good kids who had a lot of experience.

We opened the season with our traditional Columbus dual and the Kearney Invitational.

We were having success, but for some reason it felt different. It felt like we just weren't as dominant. We made more changes to the schedule and bolstered it by finishing December at the Creighton Prep Invitational before spending the entire month of January out of Nebraska with an exception, a neighborhood dual with Class B power Aurora.

We took the team to Iowa City West High School for a dual tournament in early January. In that event, we ran into perennial Illinois powerhouse Oak Park-River Forest. We were in a four-team pool and finished second to them. We won our other two duals, defeating St. James Academy of Kansas and the host school, peren-

PURPLE REIGN

nial Iowa powerhouse Iowa City West.

Iowa City West was a strong program that produced its share of NCAA Division I wrestlers and was coached by NCAA champion and former Iowa Hawkeye Mark Reiland.

The following weekend, we competed in a tournament in Newton, Kansas, where we saw such Kansas powers as Garden City, Manhattan, Arkansas City, Derby and Norton. We ran through the tournament, amassing 243 points to second-place Ark City's 178. We had 11 medalists and three champions in Javier Silva, Trey Trujillo and Billy Thompson.

We were on a roll and continuing to stockpile momentum as we moved through our schedule.

The next week, we took a much-needed break and only had a dual meet against Aurora prior to heading into the ever-challenging Top of the Rockies.

In 2013, our team had a different personality compared to some of the previous teams. We were more of a big tournament team, but with the new weight classes it helped spread out our upper weights. We had enough bigger kids that we had an advantage scoring in some of those weight classes.

At the Top of the Rockies, we were able to once again capture the team title, but by the slimmest of margins. Broomfield, a very strong 4A team, finished just two points behind us. We won 196.5-194.5 with Pomona, a strong 5A team, finishing third with 160.5 points.

The Top of the Rockies was held in two smaller adjacent gyms with very little space or seating. That, coupled with the quality of teams, made it the premier event in Colorado. It made for a stressful day just managing to move around from mat to mat with all the fans and 30-plus teams in attendance.

We managed to place seven wrestlers in the top six and once again won the tournament without an individual champion. It was an excellent test for our guys and they performed well. Andrew Rojas, Billy Thompson and Chase Reis all made the finals, but all were defeated. Jose Ceballos, Dante Rodriguez, Juan Medina and Javier Silva all medaled and set the stage for our postseason run.

HOW GRAND ISLAND BECAME A NEBRASKA WRESTLING DYNASTY

After what had become status quo, we won our conference and district titles and headed into the 2013 state tournament as the favorite. But we knew Omaha Burke would not go away easily.

We had five wrestlers advance to the state championship match that year and three were crowned champions.

Dante Rodriguez (120), Trey Trujillo (132) and Chase Reis (195) won individual state titles. We scored 180 points, 10 more than runner-up Omaha Burke in a close team race in Class A.

It was by far the closest battle we faced during our run of championships.

We knew it would be a close team race, especially when we had lost two state qualifiers and potential state medalists as we headed to state.

Sophomore upstart Billy Thompson had broken his hand during practice just days prior to the state tournament. Billy spent most of the year highly ranked and was an important cog in our lineup. We expected great things out of Billy — unfortunately we would have to wait. The injury would leave him sidelined through the state title run.

Rigo Barragan was the other state qualifier who was injured. Rigo was a junior, and late in his blood round match at districts, he twisted his knee. He finished the match, won and moved into the third-place match. At that point, we realized it was much more serious than we initially thought and he would need surgery.

We had lost two state qualifiers out of our lineup. I thought it was over and the injuries would make it nearly impossible for our team to win state again.

But the guys we did take to Omaha found a way to peak at the perfect time.

A pivotal point in the 2013 state tournament came when we went a perfect 5-for-5 in the semifinal round.

That round was huge for us and our guys really stepped up on Friday night.

That ultimately proved to be the difference for us that season.

Our wrestlers prevailed in those pressure-packed matches

PURPLE REIGN

in the semis. And it was something special to watch.

In 2013, the Grand Island Islanders made history again.

We became the first school in Class A to win five consecutive state titles since Omaha South accomplished the feat from 1956-60.

We weren't really focusing on that during the tournament, but it was still quite an accomplishment for our kids.

There had been a number of strong runs by Class A programs from Columbus, Omaha North, Lincoln East and Millard South since Omaha South had won five straight titles.

There was an abundance of components that went into that run of championships.

First and foremost, we needed talented and dedicated wrestlers. And in Class A, where team scores typically are the highest of any class at the state tournament, we needed plenty of depth.

But as anyone who has been involved in a tough, grueling sport like wrestling is aware, it is difficult to achieve your goals without being in peak physical condition.

We always did a lot of offseason wrestling. One of the guys who took advantage of every opportunity to put in time and the work in the spring and summer was Dante Rodriguez.

During that 2012-13 championship season, Dante was a junior for Grand Island and he reached his third consecutive state championship match.

He was a very gifted wrestler and a tremendous talent.

Dante would go on to qualify for the NCAA Division I tournament while wrestling for Iowa State University.

He had won a state title for Grand Island as a sophomore at 106 pounds before moving up to 120 pounds during the 2012-13 season.

Dante breezed through the first session of the 2013 state tournament with a pair of falls. He had reached the semifinals.

Those bonus points that Dante scored were huge for us. A fall was worth an additional two team points and those points can add up quickly when a team is on a roll.

We needed every point because we knew it was going to be

HOW GRAND ISLAND BECAME A NEBRASKA WRESTLING DYNASTY

a close battle in the team race.

Dante then earned a hard-fought 4-0 semifinal win over North Platte's Aaron Houser. He had reached his third straight state championship match.

Houser was coached by Dale Hall, my high school coach at Alliance my senior year. Dale had a good game plan for the match. Houser slowed us down, but it looked like he was more interested in trying to keep the match close than winning.

Dante kept his composure in the low-scoring match with Houser and took care of business.

In the finals, Dante scored a fall over Lincoln Southwest's Keegan Williams. He had pinned three of his four opponents at state. Those pins added an additional six points to our team score.

Dante put an exclamation point on an outstanding season for the Islanders.

And he had captured his second state championship while adding to his impressive collection of bonus points that he scored for us.

Dante had a tremendous career for us.

He was a fantastic wrestler and a great athlete. He accomplished a great deal in his three seasons at Grand Island.

Dante was a three-time state finalist and two-time state champion. He won a lot of big matches for us and he put on a show while doing it.

He wrestled an entertaining style, always looking to put his opponents away with a pin.

Dante also played a huge role in leading us to three state team titles in Class A.

He provided a significant spark for us at the start of our line-up.

Unfortunately, the 2013 state tournament would turn out to be the last time that Dante would wrestle for us.

Trey Trujillo was ready for redemption in 2013 after a heartbreaking end to his junior season.

He had won a state title two years before at 112 pounds before finishing second at state as a junior at 126.

PURPLE REIGN

Trey moved up to 132 pounds as a senior and returned to his winning ways when it counted most.

He was determined to finish his career on top after coming up just short at state in 2012.

Trey won his first two matches at the state tournament in 2013 before running into a familiar foe in the Class A semifinals.

He would face Omaha Creighton Prep's Hayden Hanson, the wrestler who had defeated him 4-3 in the 2012 state championship match at 126 pounds.

The rematch, as expected, was a tight, low-scoring match.

It turned into a tactical, strategical match in which Hanson did a good job of neutralizing Trey.

Neither wrestler could score a takedown in the opening two minutes and the first period ended 0-0.

Trey kept Hanson on the mat and rode him out for the entire second period. The match was still scoreless entering the final period, but we had all of the momentum.

Trey was down to start the third period and he scored an escape before earning a 1-0 win.

Trey would have liked to have opened it more, but he was an experienced wrestler who didn't become rattled in a big match.

He did what he needed to do to earn the victory.

We needed that match and Trey wrestled smart.

It was an important win for him and it was a monumental win for our team.

Getting Trey back to the finals was crucial for us. We needed every point we could get.

Trey was motivated to win that match. Their coaching staff had done a good job of slowing down Trey's explosive style.

Trey could erupt and score points in bunches. He was lethal at turning guys with the legs in. He could score a big move on his feet where he would power in on a double-leg shot and lift a guy up off the mat.

Trey came back the next day to cap his career by winning his second state championship in Class A.

He earned a wild 10-8 win over Kearney's Austin Marshall

HOW GRAND ISLAND BECAME A NEBRASKA WRESTLING DYNASTY

in the 132-pound finals.

Trey had split matches with Marshall that year heading into the finals.

That was the rubber match in the state finals.

It was a back-and-forth match, but Trey was able to score late in the third period to pull it out. He was pretty pumped up when he won.

Trey's performance was pivotal in our quest to win five consecutive state team titles.

He was a four-time state medalist, three-time finalist and two-time champ during his career with the Islanders.

And he was on four state championship teams.

He had quite a career at Grand Island.

Trey went on to wrestle at Nebraska-Kearney and then transferred to wrestle at Hastings College. He qualified for NAIA nationals.

Junior Chase Reis won our third state championship that Saturday after prevailing at 195 pounds.

Chase had a dominant tournament, winning by technical fall, fall and major decision to land a spot in the state finals. He also scored important bonus points that enabled us to win the state team title.

He capped his march by pinning Papillion-La Vista's Zach Dawe in the championship bout.

Chase had lost a tough match at state his sophomore year, so it was nice to see him come back strong.

Chase was an accomplished wrestler coming up through the youth ranks. We had high expectations for him when he was going into high school.

For him to finally win a state title, it was really exciting for us and it was inevitable.

And he scored bonus points at state with a dominant performance.

We finished with eight medalists at the 2013 state tournament and all 11 of our qualifiers were able to score points.

Our drive for five was complete.

PURPLE REIGN

And once again, it was a team effort. We needed contributions from every guy on our team that season.

Our depth was so critical during that run. Our state champions received most of the attention, but our other state medalists obviously were needed as well.

We also had state medalists in 2013 in Matt Bolan (second at 126 pounds), Edgar Silva (second at 220), John Mottl (fifth at 113), Haris Talundzic (fifth at 182) and Juan Medina (fifth at 285).

Bolan, a senior, fell to one of the state's best wrestlers in Kearney's Hunter Bamford, who captured his third state championship.

Bamford posted a 9-0 win over Matt in the 126-pound finals.

Matt placed third and second at state for us in his final two seasons. He came a long way in his career.

Early in his career, Matt only weighed 100 pounds and wrestled 112 for us because Trey Trujillo was at 103. He fought through some adversity and obstacles that season that helped him grow.

When Matt wrestled at 112 for us, we needed him to come through in the blood round at the district tournament for us to qualify all 14 weight classes for state. Matt was wrestling in Norfolk against a Norfolk wrestler. He was down late in the match and it was looking bleak for his chances. I knew Matt was in better condition.

He took the Norfolk wrestler down and brought the match within a couple of points. We elected to cut the wrestler and score takedowns. Matt scored with the same exact slide-by two or three times to force overtime in the match. And he went back to the same move by to win in OT. It was an awesome moment for Matt, as well as our team as we qualified all 14 wrestlers for state.

Matt had a good career for us and he scored a lot of big points for us at the state tournament. Winning a state title was the only milestone he didn't reach. But he still accomplished a great deal in his career.

Edgar Silva, a sophomore, earned a huge semifinal win for

us during that season. He pulled off a 4-0 upset win over Millard South's Mark Tompsett, who was ranked No. 2 at 220 and went on to win state the next season.

Edgar scored a takedown on Tompsett in the first period before adding a reversal in the third period.

He delivered for us with that win.

The takedown at the end of the first period set the tone for the match. He did a fantastic job on top and did a great job finishing that match.

Edgar then fell 6-3 in the finals against unbeaten senior and top-ranked D.J. Castillo of Lincoln High.

We were excited to see what Edgar was going to do over the next two seasons. He definitely won his share of big matches.

Juan Medina added to our list of overnight success stories at heavyweight.

Juan was a defensive tackle on the football team. I had coached him during football season and encouraged him to come out for wrestling.

He had a wrestling background, but he hadn't wrestled in more than three years.

Jeff Westerby coached him during his middle school years. Jeff knew Juan and he played a big role in convincing him to come out for wrestling.

Juan had a great season for us.

He had a lot of similar attributes that Daniel Sotelo had when Daniel wrestled for us a few years back as a senior.

Juan Medina was 6-foot-1 and started the season weighing over 300 pounds. He had to cut a little weight to make the heavyweight division. He was a big, strong kid. He wasn't as athletic as Sotelo, but he was a tough, physical competitor.

Juan was a big high school heavyweight and that worked to his advantage.

We used the same type of philosophy with Juan as we did with Daniel. We taught Juan to stay in good position and to not give up big moves. We kept the approach simple. He had to keep moving forward so he wouldn't be called for stalling. He had to score

PURPLE REIGN

from the bottom position. And he had to capitalize on the mistakes of his opponents.

Juan's decision to wrestle his senior year really paid off for us. We needed his points to win the team title.

Winning a fifth consecutive state championship was an amazing accomplishment for the Grand Island program.

It was a close, tough, hard-fought battle with a strong team from Omaha Burke.

And it was also a landmark championship for our program.

Five straight state titles separated us historically from a lot of programs.

It was a significant leap going from four to five.

We wanted to make history after our team won the first couple of times – and our athletes felt the same way.

We were shooting for the stars – that was our mentality.

We went back home to Grand Island after winning our fifth straight state title, and we had another all-school pep rally.

We marched into the gym and Queen's "We are the Champions" was blaring as our fans stood and cheered.

It was an exciting and rewarding time for our kids, our students and our community.

Those state championship celebrations never got old. It was awesome to see our wrestlers honored for what they had accomplished.

The next week, we traveled to Kearney for the inaugural Nebraska State Dual Championships. We were favored to win, but I knew without Rigo Barragan and Billy Thompson we would have holes in our lineup. We had good wrestlers that had been on our junior varsity team, but they were in for another level of wrestling.

In the first round, we soundly defeated Lincoln Southwest by a count of 57-9. In the semifinals, we ran into the always tough team from Millard South. Coach Doug Denson was prepared for us as he always was. We squeaked out a 33-32 win that put us into the finals against a very motivated Omaha Burke team.

The week after winning our fifth state title the team wasn't particularly motivated to go to Kearney for the state duals. It was

HOW GRAND ISLAND BECAME A NEBRASKA WRESTLING DYNASTY

the first time I had experienced having to motivate kids to compete again right after the state tournament. It wasn't our best week of practice. As a coaching staff, were working hard to squash the complaining while trying to prepare JV kids who hadn't wrestled in a few weeks. It was a challenging situation.

Burke thought they should have won the state tournament and they came in motivated to win the state duals. They jumped out to a huge lead on us. We were down 30-13 after they recorded falls at 145 and 152, where our starters were injured. They followed by winning decisions at 160 and 170. We bounced back with a decision at 182, a fall at 195 and two more decisions. But it wasn't quite enough. Burke edged us by a 30-27 score in the finals of the state duals.

That weekend was miserable for me. I felt like I had failed. I knew our team was better than we had performed regardless of our lineup not being at full strength. It seems like we had always overcome so many obstacles, so many times – injuries, suspensions and other changes to our lineup. On that day, Burke was better than us, but I just couldn't help but feel like I let the guys down. I didn't do enough to prepare them for it.

Was I tired? I felt like I had the answer to most every problem or adversity, but this time I didn't. I remember going home and focusing on getting back on track.

Even with the loss in the state duals, we still had plenty to be happy about.

It was never easy, even in those record-setting seasons, and that's part of the reason winning state was so special.

We ordered rings and shirts after winning our fifth straight state championship. Winning a state title was a big deal in our school and in the Grand Island community.

Every state title was special in its own way.

We had just won another championship, but I was already being asked by the media in Omaha if our streak of state titles could continue.

We returned a strong nucleus of wrestlers, so naturally people were wondering if we could win a sixth straight Class A state

PURPLE REIGN

team title in 2014.

We knew we would really have to fight, scrap and claw to do it again. We had some good kids coming back, but our depth wasn't quite as strong as it had been.

And we didn't have as many talented newcomers coming in.

But we were certainly going to try to win another state title.

Did I think it was possible?

Absolutely. But I knew we would have to be closer to perfection than ever in 2014.

CHAPTER 9
ONE FINAL TITLE

We knew our run of consecutive Class A state tournament championships might be in jeopardy as we started the 2013-14 season. We also knew we had a good nucleus of kids returning and that we were capable of making a run at a sixth straight title.

I felt like it was possible, but the margin was becoming thinner every year.

It was becoming more difficult. We didn't have as much depth as some of the better Class A teams.

We were fighting and scrapping for everything we could get.

I was nervous all season about us winning a sixth straight state championship.

There was a target on us and we were taking everybody's best shot.

We felt the same way when Millard South was on top and we were trying to knock them off.

Going into the 2013-14 season, we knew Omaha North was very talented and Millard South was very balanced. I knew it would take a near-perfect performance for us to win it.

We didn't have the superstars on the 2013-14 team that we had in the previous years.

We still had a good nucleus of wrestlers that were capable of performing at a high level.

And we knew we still had the potential to win another team

title.

The dynamics of this team had changed. The leadership wasn't as strong and the hunger had diminished.

We made a good run at it, but our string of consecutive state championships came to an end when we finished third at the 2014 state tournament in Omaha.

In a tight, lower scoring and more balanced team race than in previous years, we finished with 127 points at the Century Link Center in Omaha.

Omaha North claimed the Class A title with 156 points, holding off Millard South by just half a point.

We wrestled fairly well at state, but we lost some close matches.

We had a few tight matches where we came up short and that was devastating to us.

We had our chances, but we seemed a little snake bitten at times during the tournament.

We tried not to put too much pressure on the kids. There was a lot of talk about us going for our sixth straight title, but we didn't talk much about it with our team.

We didn't quite hit our peak that year at state.

And Omaha North and Millard South had good tournaments. Those teams wrestled well.

We had seven medalists that season, led by state finalists Andrew Rojas at 138 pounds and Chase Reis at 220.

Rojas dropped a 7-4 decision in the finals to Millard South sophomore Isaac DeLoa, who would go on to win four state titles.

Reis lost by fall to Millard South's Marc Tompsett in the finals. Tompsett pinned his way through the state tournament.

Chase was undefeated all year and nobody could stop him.

He was on the all-tournament team at The Clash and won the Top of the Rockies.

He was wrestling at a very high level.

And he was going to be tough to beat.

Chase was heavily favored to win that match against Tompsett, but he was caught on his back early in the match.

And we were stunned.

The Millard South crowd went crazy and we were deflated.

My heart was just broken for Chase.

He was the All-American kid who was just nice to everybody. He was a good, upstanding young man and a hard-working student.

He was a kid who did everything right.

Chase wrestled like a middleweight even though he was in a bigger weight class. He was athletic and had a good arsenal of moves.

Chase had made his third straight state final after winning a 2013 state title at 195 pounds. He placed second at 170 pounds in 2012.

It is unfortunate that Chase came up short of winning state as a senior.

Chase finished his career as a three-time state finalist.

Chase Reis could've wrestled at the small college level. Instead, he chose to play football in college at Morningside College in Sioux City, Iowa.

He had an outstanding college career, earning all-conference honors for a team that went 15-0 and won the NAIA national football championship in 2018. It was Morningside's first NAIA title.

Reis was named Defensive Player of the Game in his team's 35-28 win over Benedictine (Kansas) in the national title game. He had eight tackles in the game, including a sack and 2½ tackles for losses.

Chase was one of the leaders on our Grand Island Senior High wrestling team in 2014.

We also had medalists that year in Billy Thompson (third at 170), Edgar Silva (third at 195), Skylar Schmidt (fifth at 113), Dante Todd (fifth at 132) and Rigo Barragan (sixth at 145).

It was disappointing to see our streak of consecutive state championships end. We felt like we had a chance to keep it going, but we just didn't get it done.

Deep down, I had a few doubts going into that state tournament.

We had struggled trying to get the team to reach its peak and I

PURPLE REIGN

feel responsible for not getting it done.

It was tough to see it end.

I feel like I could've done more.

There were a number of factors why it didn't happen.

It was disappointing and frustrating.

I feel like I let the kids down and didn't get them in position to get the job done.

We were without a two-time returning state champion and three-time state finalist that season.

Dante Rodriguez, who placed second at state in 2011 before winning back-to-back state titles for Grand Island in 2012 and 2013, transferred to Kearney High School for his senior season.

Dante had grown up in Kearney, but started high school at Grand Island Senior High when it looked like he wouldn't be able to make Kearney's starting lineup as a freshman.

Returning state champion Hunter Bamford was coming back for Kearney in 2011. Dante made the state finals for us a freshman before losing to Bamford in the finals.

To nobody's surprise, Dante continued his winning ways when he left Grand Island.

He won his third state title in 2014, capturing the Class A championship for Kearney at 132 pounds. He went unbeaten, recording three falls and a technical fall at his final state tournament.

Dante finished his prep career as a four-time state finalist and a three-time state champion. He had a 155-16 career record at the high school level.

I wish he would've finished his prep career where he started.

Dante went on to wrestle at the NCAA Division I level for Iowa State University, where he qualified for the NCAA Championships for the Cyclones. He also was a Big 12 runner-up for Iowa State.

He finished his college career at Northern Colorado.

I'm not saying we would have won the 2014 state team title with Dante in our lineup that year, but we certainly would've been in the championship hunt.

I was shocked when I heard that Dante was planning to leave Grand Island.

I couldn't believe it. He had spent three years with us. He benefited by being a part of a strong program and we benefited by having a wrestler of his caliber in our lineup.

I found out during the end of his junior year in the spring of 2013 that Dante had decided he was going back to Kearney for his senior year of high school.

He was still in school in Grand Island for a few more weeks before the school year ended.

His family's reasoning was that he wanted to go to school with his brother, who had won a couple of state medals for Kearney Catholic.

Dante thrived during his time at Grand Island Senior High. We had an experienced coaching staff and he also had plenty of top wrestlers to train with.

It felt like we were being betrayed when I heard he was leaving.

It was disappointing.

I do know his family made a lot of sacrifices for him to wrestle for us and go to school in Grand Island. And I know they spent a lot of money driving back and forth between Kearney and Grand Island.

It was strange looking across the mat and seeing Dante wrestling for another team during his senior season.

We dualed Kearney High a couple of times during the 2013-14 season and we wrestled against them at the Kearney Invite. We saw Dante quite a bit that year.

If you throw another 20 or 25 points in there from Dante, we probably would have been right up there in contention at the state tournament in 2014.

Who knows how it might have all played out?

We believed we could've still won state without Dante, but it didn't happen.

It wasn't the first time something like this had happened to us.

We also had lost state champion Alec Chanthapatheth for his

PURPLE REIGN

senior season in high school and we didn't have two-time state champion Blake Fruchtl for his last two state tournaments.

Even with all of the adversity we faced, we had some amazing success with our wrestling program.

But the level of success wasn't as good as it could have been if we would have had some of those kids who didn't quite finish.

That's part of coaching. And it happens to every program.

There are a million things that have to be managed and a million things that can derail a team.

We had a few of those derailments, but we were able to keep the train on the tracks.

We had guys step in and step up. The depth we built was a huge part of our success.

It was still a solid performance by our team that year and those kids had nothing to feel bad about.

They were part of something pretty remarkable.

What we did during those years, winning five straight state tournament championships, is something to be extremely proud of.

I was proud of our program, our kids, our community, our school and everybody that was with us and behind us. We had great support.

It was a blast seeing our kids and our team achieve their lofty goals.

Our streak of state tournament titles had come to an end, but we still had a chance to finish the season with a state championship trophy.

The Nebraska School Activities Association added the state wrestling duals in 2013 and we reached the Class A finals before falling 30-27 to Omaha Burke.

We were missing two key starters when we lost to Burke. One match would've changed the outcome of that dual.

What made it worse is that we had beaten Burke early that season.

After coming up short in Omaha at the 2014 state tournament, we had a chance a week later at the state duals. The event was held at the University of Nebraska at Kearney.

HOW GRAND ISLAND BECAME A NEBRASKA WRESTLING DYNASTY

It was a chore to bring the team back to wrestle in the state duals the week after the traditional state tournament.

Our whole season revolved around preparing for the state tournament in Omaha. And we had fallen short of our goal of winning another team title.

I knew trying to prepare our team for the state duals in 2014 was going to be challenging.

I told our wrestlers to take the Monday off after the state tournament.

And then I met with the team on Tuesday.

"What do you want to do?" I asked our guys. "I'm pissed off that we didn't win the state tournament and I want to do something about it. I want to win the state duals.

"We need a couple tough days of practice. It ain't going to be easy and it ain't going to be fun. But I believe we can win the state duals."

The kids were on board, so we got after it and we had a couple of good, hard days of practice.

Our kids focused on the state duals.

That week of practice was better than it was the year before when we competed at the first state duals.

We came out strong when the competition started.

We opened the Class A state duals by rolling past Hastings 56-12 in the quarterfinal round.

Next was a tough semifinal matchup against traditional power Kearney. We came through to win that dual 41-27.

We forfeited to Kearney senior Dante Rodriguez, who had won two state titles and finished second for us at Grand Island during his first three years of high school.

We wrestled well in the dual against Kearney and earned a hard-fought win against them.

We advanced to the final round against perennial power and long-time nemesis Millard South.

Coach Doug Denson's team was determined and motivated to win the state duals after Omaha North had edged them by half a point to win the traditional state tournament the week before.

PURPLE REIGN

We knew it was going to be a tough dual. Doug was an excellent coach who was very good at adjusting his lineups to maximize his chances in a dual meet.

We learned that first-hand when we dropped a big dual meet against them a few years before. He had shifted some wrestlers around in their lineup and the strategy had paid off for Millard South.

The starting weight for the 2014 state championship dual meet between Grand Island and Millard South, by random draw, was at 220 pounds.

I had learned from Doug that dual meets sometimes are like chess matches. You are trying to take the pieces you have and best use them to your advantage.

We shifted our lineup around to try and find the best matchup possible. And it worked out beautifully.

We decided to bump both Edgar Silva and Chase Reis up a weight class and it paid big dividends for us.

Silva posted a 6-2 decision over Marc Tompsett, the same wrestler who had defeated Reis in the Class A 220-pound championship match at the state tournament the week before. That was a huge win for us and that set the tone for the rest of the dual.

Reis followed by earning a 9-1 major decision over Terry Jeub at heavyweight.

As bad as Reis wanted a rematch with Tompsett, he was more than willing to move up a weight class to help the team.

And Chase Reis came through by earning a bonus point for the team when he won by a major decision.

He delivered a clutch win for us.

The team always came first during my days in Grand Island and never was that more evident than on this day.

Millard South came back when Nathan Rodriguez downed Miguel Hernandez 7-1 at 106 pounds.

We were able to respond to that setback when Skylar Schmidt pinned Austin Coufal in 2 minutes, 45 seconds at 113 to give us an early 13-3 lead.

Our crowd erupted as we grabbed the early momentum in the

dual meet.

That pin was huge for us. We knew we needed every point.

We figured the dual was close and may come down to the final few matches.

Millard South won the next two bouts before Dante Todd came through for us and delivered a big pin over Connor Olin at 132 pounds.

Another pin meant another six team points for us.

The meet continued to be close. Andrew Rojas won by forfeit for us at 145 and Billy Thompson rolled to a 15-0 win by technical fall at 170. It was Billy's 100th career win.

With two matches to go, the scoreboard read:

Grand Island 30
Millard South 23

The next match at 182 pounds would be critical and the fate of the dual likely would hinge on its outcome.

We would be sending Gage Grinnell onto the mat for the biggest match of his career. Gage was a sophomore who had wrestled a few varsity matches, but he had competed mainly on the junior varsity that season.

But Gage wrestled like a seasoned veteran when he delivered a huge 11-8 win over Millard South's Dylan Kuehn in their 182-pound bout.

Earlier in the day, Gage had earned a pin over Kearney's Jake Culey during our 41-27 victory over the Bearcats in the semifinal round.

We needed Gage in our last two duals and he came through. He earned two big wins for us. He did a great job and he showed the moxie so many previous GI backup wrestlers had when called upon.

Gage started the match with Kuehn by being taken down and nearly put on his back by the Millard South wrestler.

Gage showed plenty of resiliency. He came right back, scoring a takedown and two near-fall points to lead 7-5 after the first period.

He still had a two-point lead, 9-7, late in the match before

PURPLE REIGN

scoring a takedown in the third period to put it away.

That sealed the win for Gage and enabled us to become the Class A state dual meet champions.

Our bench and our fans went crazy. We were all cheering, yelling, high-fiving and hugging.

Gage really came through to give us an exciting win over a very good Millard South team.

We earned a thrilling 33-29 win in a hard-fought battle. It was an awesome way to end our season.

A big key for us in that dual was the majority of the matches came down to our kids not giving up many bonus points.

We had some matches in which we had to keep the score close and keep them down so our big scorers could score big points for us.

Our kids deserve a ton of credit for their effort on that day.

Our whole bench jumped in the air when Gage Grinnell won.

There was a big emotional release from our team.

We vindicated ourselves from the week before and showed we were the best dual team in the state.

This was the recap of the Class A state duals final in 2014:

Grand Island 33, Millard South 29

220 pounds – Edgar Silva, GI, dec. Marc Tompsett, MS, 6-2; 285 – Chase Reis, GI, maj. dec. Terry Jeub, MS, 9-1; 106 – Nathan Rodriguez, MS, dec. Miguel Hernandez, GI, 7-1; 113 – Skylar Schmidt, GI, pinned Austin Coufal, MS, 2:45; 120 – Ryan Kostszewa, MS, dec. Blake Coen, GI, 7-1; 126 – Zac Charity, MS, pinned Nick Sheldon, GI, 2:26; 132 – Dante Todd, GI, pinned Connor Olin, MS, 2:59; 138 – Isaac DeLoa, MS, tech fall over Chris Doty, GI, 15-0; 145 – Andrew Rojas, GI, won by forfeit; 152 – Alex Mendez, MS, dec. Rigo Barragan, GI, 3-1; 160 – Tyler Calder, MS, dec. Jared Fortune, GI, 6-4; 170 – Billy Thompson, GI, tech fall over Gavyn Angerman, MS, 15-0; 182 – Gage Grinnell, GI, dec. Dylan Kuehn, MS, 11-8; 195 – Anthony Cloyd, MS, won by forfeit.

The state duals provided another way for the senior class of Rojas, Reis, Jared Fortune, Barragan and Kasey Townsend to go out on top.

Grinnell went on to win a state championship for Grand Island two years later. He won a Class A title at 285 pounds in 2016.

Gage won two matches by fall and one by major decision en route to his state title.

Gage also went on to play football in college at Morningside.

Winning the state duals in 2014 provided a perfect opportunity for redemption for our team and for our program. And it provided Grand Island with another way to win a state championship.

We had won a state team title in wrestling for the sixth straight season after winning the traditional state tournament five straight times from 2009-13, and then adding the state duals title in 2014.

Our kids felt really good about what happened. The kids came back a week after the state tournament and redeemed themselves at the state duals.

The seniors deserved it because their class still was able to be four-time state champs. Maybe it wasn't quite the way we wanted it to be, but they still were on top every year they were in high school.

It was a state championship nonetheless, and that felt pretty good.

Winning in a dual-meet format was exciting because the entire team was involved and the fans were into every match.

That state duals championship would be my final event as the head wrestling coach at Grand Island Senior High.

I accepted an offer to return to the collegiate level as the head coach at nearby Hastings College. Hastings competed at the NAIA level.

I had some connections at Hastings and I knew a few people on their football staff.

Jerry Schmutte, the athletic director at Hastings, called me and made a strong pitch to bring me in as their next head wrestling coach.

I drove down there and he took me out for supper. It was pretty informal and relaxed. We talked and got to know each other.

Eventually, he offered me the position.

PURPLE REIGN

"I'm not going to pull any punches," Schmutte told me. "I want you to be our next wrestling coach."

Jerry and I hit it off. He was a no-nonsense guy and he liked the traits and the work ethic that I exhibited as a coach.

I never thought I would have a chance to coach in college again after I left Dakota Wesleyan, but this was an opportunity for me to go back to that level.

I was doing well at Grand Island and I was making a great living. But the offer to go back to college coaching was too good to pass up.

Hastings made me a strong offer and I talked it over with my wife before accepting.

Hastings was only a short, 30-minute drive from Grand Island, so I wouldn't have to relocate.

I jumped into my new job at Hastings College right away and didn't have time to reflect on what we had done at Grand Island.

We had a heck of a run at Grand Island Senior High. We had our share of challenges and obstacles to overcome during my time there from 2003-14.

It might have looked easy at times, but it was never easy. Wrestling is a tough, demanding, grueling sport that is difficult even when you are winning.

We were fortunate to have our fair share of success and we definitely saw an abundance of kids find direction in their lives because of their involvement in the sport of wrestling.

I was fortunate and blessed to be a part of numerous accomplishments during my 11 seasons with the Grand Island Islanders program.

We won five straight Class A state tournament championships from 2009-13.

We also captured the championship at the Class A state duals in 2014.

We set what still remains the Class A state tournament scoring record of 252.5 points in 2009. And we tied the all-class record with 12 state medalists that season.

Our wrestlers combined to win 21 individual state champi-

HOW GRAND ISLAND BECAME A NEBRASKA WRESTLING DYNASTY

onships and 83 state medals during my 11 seasons as the head coach for the Islanders. We finished in the state's top 10 in all but one of my 11 seasons at Grand Island.

We had the school's first four-time state champion in Andrew Riedy along with a four-time state finalist in Carlos Rodriguez.

Two other wrestlers I coached – Blake Fruchtl and Dante Rodriguez – each won three state titles.

We had six different wrestlers win at least two state titles.

Our teams won nearly 80 percent of our duals. We were 156-41 during my time with the Islanders.

Our teams captured eight district titles and eight conference titles.

I was named Nebraska state coach of the year three times and was a finalist for national coach of the year.

I was humbled and excited to learn that I had been selected for induction into the Grand Island Senior High Athletics Hall of Fame.

It is a prestigious honor that I am incredibly grateful and proud to receive.

A large part of the credit for the success we had obviously goes to the young men who dedicated themselves to the Grand Island program and bought into what we were trying to do.

Our athletes worked and trained extremely hard to become an elite program. We built a winning culture where success became contagious and spread like wildfire among the young men who competed for us.

Their year-round dedication and commitment enabled many of their dreams to turn into reality.

We also had an excellent group of assistant coaches who made major contributions as well.

Geoff Cyboron, Les Aguilar, Rob Riedy, Jeff Westerby, Matt Sedivy, Larry Lucas, Joe Grenier, Kevin Watson, Dan Carlson and Jeff South were among the assistants who did a great job for us.

There is no way we could have accomplished what we did without the enormous amount of time and effort they put into our wrestling program.

PURPLE REIGN

We were fortunate to have some excellent coaches on our staff and that made a big difference with our program.

We had good guys who were always on the same page with what we wanted to achieve. We had a lot of the same philosophies and approaches.

Every one of them made unique contributions and developed strong relationships with the kids.

Building those relationships was important in achieving the level of success that we had.

We also had very good administrative support during my time at Grand Island. That made a big difference. Anybody who has been a head coach fully understands the importance of having the support and backing it takes to build a successful program.

We also were fortunate and blessed to have great facilities at our school.

There are so many components involved in building a championship program and we had everything in place at Grand Island to be successful.

I left a strong team behind at Grand Island when I left for Hastings College. We had built a culture of winning and that had filtered down into the kids' programs in Grand Island.

There were still a number of top wrestlers still competing at the high school level.

The first year after I left, the 2015 Islanders team placed second at the state tournament in Class A under first-year head coach Joey Morrison.

Billy Thompson (170) and Edgar Silva (195) won individual state titles that season.

Millard South won the team title with 172.5 points and Grand Island finished second with 154.5 points in 2015.

I knew they had an opportunity to have a very good season. They had a number of top wrestlers returning.

Billy Thompson and Edgar Silva were motivated to come back and have strong seasons. And they did just that. I was happy to see them achieve their goals and earn spots on the top of the medal podium.

HOW GRAND ISLAND BECAME A NEBRASKA WRESTLING DYNASTY

Grand Island didn't have the top-to-bottom talent that we had in those previous years, but they had a very good state tournament.

Millard South was rebuilding and reloading. And preparing to go on another championship run.

The Islanders continued to excel after placing fourth at state in Class A in 2016.

Those were exciting times for Grand Island wrestling.

The program enjoyed a remarkable run of success at a school that provided me with so many special memories.

It was enjoyable to be a part of it.

CHAPTER 10
BACK TO COLLEGE

Leaving Grand Island Senior High for Hastings College wasn't an easy decision. We had built a very strong and successful wrestling program at Grand Island and that was evident the year after I left.

With a number of top wrestlers back from my final team, the Islanders went on to have another excellent season.

It was tough to leave the Grand Island program. I had some great memories from my time as the head coach there and it was not easy to say goodbye, especially to some of the kids who were still competing for the Islanders.

I always wanted to just coach at the college level. That was my goal after I finished my own competitive career as an athlete at Adams State.

And that's what happened when I was hired as the coach at Dakota Wesleyan shortly after I finished school.

After I left Dakota Wesleyan in 2003 and took the job at Grand Island Senior High, I got married, had kids and earned another master's degree. I was doing well on the pay scale, so I wasn't sure I would ever coach at the college level again.

We had a well-established program at Grand Island that had gone on an unprecedented run of success.

But then the opportunity came up to be a college coach again and I couldn't pass it up.

I coached just three seasons at Hastings College. I coached

PURPLE REIGN

one All-American during my time there with two other wrestlers that I recruited going on to become NAIA All-Americans after I left the school.

Hastings athletic director Jerry Schmutte hired me in 2014, but Jerry decided to step down from his position just a few months after he brought me into the school. It was announced in January 2015 that Schmutte would be leaving his post as athletic director that June.

I knew that Jerry was an older guy, and I knew he might not be around that long after he hired me, but I didn't expect him to hang it up that soon.

I felt like I had been sold a bill of goods at Dakota Wesleyan. They didn't follow through on a lot of the promises they made to me when I was hired.

Hastings College made a lot of similar promises to me when I was hired and I trusted that they were going to follow through.

Jerry sold me on Hastings and had me believing we could do big things there. He convinced me that he would follow through on providing me the support and resources I needed to be successful.

But it didn't take long to figure out that after Jerry left Hastings that a lot of promises he made weren't going to be delivered to me and the wrestling program.

A number of my Grand Island wrestlers followed me and competed for me at Hastings College.

My first season at Hastings, we had three wrestlers qualify for the NAIA Championships in 2015.

Two of them – Alec Chanthapatheth (141 pounds) and Trey Trujillo (133) – had won state championships for me at Grand Island Senior High. Alec went 1-2 at nationals and Trey went 0-2 that season.

Trey Trujillo was one of two Hastings wrestlers to qualify for nationals the following season for us in 2016. He went 1-2 at the national tournament and came up short of the medal podium.

When I took over as the head coach at Hastings, we were limited on numbers. We only had 15 kids and very little depth. It was a struggle from the beginning.

HOW GRAND ISLAND BECAME A NEBRASKA WRESTLING DYNASTY

I was trying to bring in kids and build our numbers. And establish some depth.

The Hastings program didn't have a good reputation when I took over. There had been issues with wrestlers struggling in school and getting in trouble off the mat.

The wrestling program had a bad reputation around campus and in the community.

We tried to change that perception and bring in better students and better citizens.

We were able to do that and we started to see some improvement in all areas of the program.

My third season at Hastings saw us land a wrestler on the podium and give me my first All-American during my short time there.

I started recruiting kids from California junior colleges and it was paying off.

I had some connections in California from my days as a college wrestler. And I also knew some of the high school coaches. There were a lot of good wrestlers in California looking for an opportunity to wrestle in college.

One of the wrestlers we landed was Jeremiah Gerl, from Long Beach, California. It took some time, but we eventually convinced him to come to Hastings and wrestle for us.

We signed a number of kids from California, three of whom became All-Americans at Hastings.

Jeremiah Gerl qualified for nationals during the first season he wrestled for us. He was a junior during the 2016-17 school year after transferring to Hastings.

Jeremiah came from a huge and close-knit Christian family. They were great people to be around and they reminded me of a lot of families I knew from the Midwest. They had strong values and beliefs.

Jeremiah fit in well when he arrived at Hastings College. He wasn't the most talented wrestler, but he more than made up for that in a number of other ways. He believed in his abilities. He had no shortage of confidence. He was a great leader by example and he

PURPLE REIGN

was a hard worker.

Jeremiah was a tough wrestler. He would wear people down with his physical style of wrestling.

He was a good leg rider who pinned people and he was just a hard-nosed brawler who would break people by keeping them down on the mat.

I didn't think Jeremiah was quite good enough to make the podium that year at the national tournament. I wasn't sure that he was at that level yet and I thought maybe he was a year away from making a run at All-American honors.

But he was a confident kid with a strong belief in his own abilities. And he surprised us with a great performance.

Jeremiah won his first two matches at the 2017 NAIA national tournament to advance to the semifinal round at 197 pounds.

He had clinched All-American honors and had clinched a top-six finish.

Gerl then dropped a 5-2 decision to top-ranked Dalton Bailey of Life University in the semifinals.

It was a good match. Bailey was an athletic, funky wrestler who could really scramble. It was a clash of styles. Jeremiah wrestled hard, but he didn't have quite enough in his arsenal to overcome a talented opponent of Bailey's caliber.

Jeremiah showed plenty of resolve and fight when he was able to battle back to defeat No. 2 John Hensley of Great Falls 2-1 in the consolation semifinals.

It was a great match, and Jeremiah was able to keep the guy on the mat to secure the victory.

That win clinched a top-four finish for Jeremiah, which was huge for our program.

Jeremiah then dropped a hard-fought, strategical 1-0 decision to No. 4 John Dennis of Grand View in the third-place match.

Jeremiah Gerl finished fourth to become the school's fourth All-American and the first since 2014. It was the highest finish at nationals in Hastings College school history.

We were happy to have an All-American. It validated what we

were doing.

We felt like we were headed in the right direction and Jeremiah's finish had given the program a significant boost.

We were on the verge of doing some good things at Hastings College.

Gerl came back to place third at nationals the following season at heavyweight.

We also had finished a respectable third in the conference in 2017, and we qualified four wrestlers for the national tournament.

About the time we were starting to build the program and have success on the national level, I ran into the same problem that I had dealt with years before at Dakota Wesleyan.

Hastings College wanted to reduce my salary.

Two months after the season ended, I was forced to make another tough decision – stay at Hastings for less pay or move on.

On May 16, 2017, I announced my resignation as the head wrestling coach at Hastings.

This was the statement I issued in the press release that announced my departure from the school:

"I am very appreciative for the opportunity to meet my professional goals of successfully leading a collegiate wrestling program. I wish nothing but the best for the student-athletes, the new coaches and the program."

Hastings athletic director Patty Sitorius shared her thoughts on my resignation in the same press release:

"On behalf of Hastings College, I want to thank Coach Schadwinkel for his tireless service to Hastings College and to the wrestling program. We will certainly miss Mike's commitment and leadership but know that his drive for excellence will help him to succeed in his future endeavors. Coach Schadwinkel has been given a wonderful opportunity outside of athletics and I have no doubt he will be nothing but successful."

It would have been difficult for me to continue at Hastings for less pay. I had a family to support and the pay cut wasn't going to work for me.

I could've stayed at Hastings through July 2018 and made the

PURPLE REIGN

same salary before taking the pay cut.

They were happy with the job I was doing at Hastings, but they were going to have to cut my salary.

We had already gone through scholarship and budget reductions, but I still felt like we could build something even with those limitations.

I felt like I could consistently produce All-Americans and contend for conference titles. I knew we could still win, and I could be a good mentor to young men and serve the school in a strong capacity.

But I felt betrayed, hurt and disappointed when they told me they were going to cut my salary.

We were on track to accomplish some really good things for Hastings College.

I felt like my career was being ripped away from me. And that obviously was very frustrating for me.

I left the success that we had at Grand Island to go to Hastings and then they decide I was not worth the salary they were paying me.

I very bitter and angry. It was disheartening. And it was upsetting.

It was a bitter pill to swallow.

But I also learned there was another job opening that I had an interest in pursuing.

I applied for the athletic director job at Grand Island Senior High in the spring of 2017.

I interviewed for the job at Grand Island and I thought it went well. I thought I had a good chance to land the position.

When I received the call that I didn't get the job, my heart sank. I thought I was supposed to get that job, but it went to another strong candidate.

Cindy Wells, a long-time employee at Grand Island Senior High, was hired to replace Joe Kutlas as athletic director.

Cindy had been an assistant principal at Grand Island Senior High. She also had been the volleyball coach.

I was disappointed that I didn't get the job, but Cindy was

someone with strong credentials who had been at Grand Island for many years.

My wife, Kelli, was extremely supportive during that time as I weighed my options.

"We will figure it out," she said, "and we will make it work."

Kelli calmed me down and helped me during that time.

At the time, I still had the option of staying at Hastings with the same pay for one more year before my salary would be cut.

But around that time, another opportunity presented itself.

I was friends with Rod Shada, who had been a great mentor and a great friend to me. Rod had been the long-time wrestling coach at Grand Island, whose team won a Class A state title in 1973.

Rod was working as a counselor at Grand Island Senior High during my time as the wrestling coach there. He was a big supporter of mine and I appreciated that.

I had called Rod's son, Damon, to see how his father was doing.

At the end of the conversation, Damon asked me how it was going at Hastings.

I explained my situation and then told him I might be looking for something new.

"If there's anything you have available," I said, "let me know."

Damon immediately responded by saying that he did have something I might be interested in. He worked for Truck Center Companies in York, Nebraska.

Damon reached out to Chad Kelsay, who is vice president of sales for the company. Shortly after, Chad contacted me.

Chad Kelsay played football for the University of Nebraska and in the National Football League.

They offered me a contract and I accepted a position working in sales for Truck Center Companies in York, Nebraska.

Trey Mytty, whose father Guy was the legendary wrestling coach at Tekamah-Herman, is the president and CEO of Truck Center Companies.

PURPLE REIGN

Trey wrestled and is a huge fan and supporter of the sport.

Trey does a great job of taking care of the people who work for him.

When I left coaching in May 2017, it was a whirlwind during that time and happened quickly.

When I resigned from Hastings, I was officially stepping away from coaching.

Teaching and coaching were the only professions that I had known.

Some of the kids at Hastings College were disappointed that I was leaving and I understood that. They didn't know all of the circumstances. It was difficult for me to have to leave those kids.

I had no plans to leave Hastings before they told me they were going to cut my salary.

We were building something with the program and I wanted to see that through, especially with the kids that I had recruited.

But I really couldn't afford to stay.

The year after I left, Hastings had three All-Americans and placed in the top 15 in the country as a team in 2018 with kids that I had recruited.

It was a tough decision to leave Hastings, especially when you consider that I had been a head wrestling coach at the college and high school level for 18 years.

It's tough to make a career change when you are over 40 years old.

But that is what I did.

I love what I'm doing now. I'm working for a great company and I love the people I work for.

It's been a fun job – it's very different from what I was used to doing.

I left the educational world to move into the corporate world.

It was completely new and foreign to me, but the transition has gone well.

My wife works in Lincoln, about a 45-minute drive across Interstate 80 from where I work in York. We found a place to live in between the two cities.

HOW GRAND ISLAND BECAME A NEBRASKA WRESTLING DYNASTY

We settled on living in Seward, a town of around 7,000 people. We like it there and our family has transitioned well.

The proximity to Lincoln and Omaha are great for us. And we still have the smaller town and smaller schools in Seward, which we like.

Seward is a little bit smaller than where I grew up in Alliance, but similar in size.

My wife has done well in her career and she has a great job. She is a statewide juvenile probation administrator in the state probation offices in Lincoln.

Settling in Seward has worked out well for us and we both have fairly short commutes to work.

Looking back on my coaching career, it's been an adventure as I've gone from college coaching to the high school level and then back to college again.

I have so many fond and lasting memories from my time as a wrestling coach, particularly during my time at Grand Island.

It was amazing to be a part of five straight Class A state tournament championships.

And it was awesome to see my final team win the state duals.

Those kids were so resilient, bouncing back in 2014 after our string of state tournament titles had ended.

Those glory days in Grand Island were surreal. It's hard to imagine that really happened.

It blows my mind when I think back on it. I knew we would be good, but I didn't know we would be that good and that it would be that sustainable. We had some great kids who performed when it counted.

It was a lot of fun. We had an interesting dynamic. We had wrestlers coming out of our kids' club and we also had kids who came out for wrestling in high school who didn't have much exposure.

It was a great run and a magical ride.

I will never forget it.

CHAPTER 11
HOW DID IT HAPPEN?

I've been asked in many arenas by many different people how I did it at Grand Island. My first response is I didn't do it, but it was a perfect storm. So many factors were just right to create the success of Grand Island's wrestling program.

It started with great coaches before me. Rod Shada and then Kurt Frohling laid an amazing foundation for me when I took over.

The administrative support was excellent.

I have mentioned many times that having Dr. Mann and his staff of athletic-minded administrators gave me the flexibility to succeed. They allowed me the freedom to work at my teaching job and pour energy into it as well as coaching. They gave me the ability to do both jobs well.

Joe Kutlas was more than a boss. He was a friend, a mentor, a confidant and a motivator. Joe allowed me to take nearly full control of every aspect of the wrestling program. I couldn't have asked for a better athletic director to allow me to be a great as I wanted to be. He gave me the resources, the staff and nearly anything I felt I needed to build our program. I am forever indebted to him professionally.

The feeder programs in place upon my arrival were the next big catalyst to this perfect storm. Rob Riedy was in the middle of just starting Team GI and rallying dads, former wrestlers and a team of people to build a youth program.

PURPLE REIGN

It paid off with the countless number of wrestlers who came through that program becoming state medalists and state champions.

Another feeder program was already in place with the Islander Wrestling Club. It fed the program for decades prior to my arrival. The work of Jeff Westerby in our toughest, low-income middle school also provided a huge boost for us.

Jeff always was scouring the halls of Walnut Middle School for his next project athlete. Isaiah Aguilar, Tyler Glover, Alec Chanthapatheth, Jose Ceballos, and Jeff and Jason Brisbin were among the state qualifiers, medalists and champions that may have never been exposed to wrestling had it not been for Jeff.

Philosophically, we wanted every kid to be a multiple sport athlete.

If a wrestler was out for track, baseball or soccer in the spring, they would participate in that.

Every wrestler that wasn't out for a spring sport, I wanted them doing strength and conditioning with me.

They had to be doing something to stay in shape and to help them prepare for the following season.

A lot of our upper weight wrestlers also played football. I tried to recruit football players to wrestle. In many cases, we had a lot of success with that.

We had a number of big success stories where our heavyweights excelled in wrestling after we talked them into joining the team.

Two-time state champion Carlos Rodriguez was a two-sport athlete who played baseball for Grand Island. Wrestling was definitely his sport, but he also was a good baseball player.

We had a good strength program called Islander Power with John Swanson. John did a great job and he built a specific program for the wrestlers to follow in the offseason.

He had two programs for his athletes to follow and we had our wrestlers do the tougher one.

We also had open mat workouts, usually two or three days a week, where our guys could come in and wrestle on their own.

HOW GRAND ISLAND BECAME A NEBRASKA WRESTLING DYNASTY

The open mat workouts were available for the kids almost year-round.

The kids would also take advantage of the open workouts to prepare for freestyle and Greco-Roman wrestling competitions during that time.

There were numerous tournaments around the area and the region during the spring. There also were a few national tournaments, including the Cadet and Junior Nationals each July in Fargo, North Dakota.

We asked our wrestlers to come in and lift weights four times a week during the summer.

We started a Wednesday night summer league, similar to what Coach Mike Denney was doing at Division II college powerhouse Nebraska-Omaha.

We had a lot of kids wrestling in the league.

Local college clinicians came in to provide instruction to our wrestlers.

We made some money from the Wednesday night league and then poured all of it back into the program.

We hosted summer camps and brought in some big names to provide instruction and insight.

Tolly Thompson, an NCAA champion for Nebraska and a world bronze medalist, was among those we brought in for our camps. Tolly's wife was from Grand Island, so that worked out great for us. He would work a camp and then his family would come back to Grand Island to visit.

We also were very fortunate to have Bryan Snyder, James Green and Jason Powell from the University of Nebraska help with our camps.

Snyder was a two-time NCAA finalist who became the top assistant coach for the Huskers. Green was an All-American at Nebraska who went on to become a two-time world medalist. Powell won an NCAA title for Nebraska before joining the coaching staff at his alma mater.

It was awesome to learn from guys with their high level of experience and expertise.

PURPLE REIGN

We had Nebraska-Kearney coach Marc Bauer come over as well. Marc coached UNK to three national titles in Division II. Marc has an upbeat, positive personality and he related very well to the kids.

We were fortunate to have good clinicians come in and that made a big difference.

We weren't able to pay them a lot of money, so we were very appreciative that they took time out of their busy schedules.

We had a lot of kids from around our area come in to Grand Island for our league and camps. It was an excellent opportunity for them to wrestle some good competition.

We would usually have around 100 kids in our summer league.

It provided a way for our kids to learn, grow and develop. And it kept them on the mat during the summer.

We also took a lot of kids to the University of Nebraska wrestling camp. Husker coach Mark Manning and his staff were fantastic to me and the kids in our program. They were always very accommodating to the Grand Island teams.

We hosted state USA Wrestling and AAU events in Grand Island. And we hosted the Huskerland state dual tournament.

We were able to make money on those events that went back into the program. That money created opportunities for our kids to go to camps and compete in events where there were travel expenses involved.

We were trying to give our kids every opportunity to improve during the spring and summer.

Wrestling is a sport that takes an incredible time commitment for success.

I always believed that wrestling a tough schedule was most beneficial for our program, especially when we started to dominate. I knew that it was more about helping our kids reach their potential than it was about merely winning. Going through tough times makes you a stronger person and when you need that strength, it will be there because of those tough times.

Wrestling doesn't necessarily need more tough times to build character. It naturally provides it. But if you are winning all of the time and not facing any adversity, then as a coach, I believed I needed to provide it. That is why I believed our program was ready and needed a greater challenge in scheduling when we won our first state title. Thankfully, Joe Kutlas, our administration and our booster club were on board with out-of-state travel.

The mental side of wrestling has always been a part of my coaching. Watching kids like Isaiah Aguilar, who initially didn't believe in himself, achieve at our highest level is unforgettable. I always believed in my kids. I trusted that I had them ready physically, so the only reason they should ever lack confidence is from not preparing mentally.

I struggled through learning strategies on my own throughout my competitive career. I tried to always make sure our kids were mentally ready to compete. Admittedly, I wasn't perfect, but having those mental strategies builds confidence. Without confidence, I believe wrestlers are limited to only physical ability which we all know will only take a person so far.

Creating a pre-match routine to make sure a wrestler is ready to compete is baseline duty as a coach. I wanted kids to build confidence in their preparation. Each guy had to have his own system of getting himself warmed up physically and his own way of building confidence mentally.

Two of the best mental strategies are through mental imagery and self-talk. Mental imagery is helping your athlete to envision success prior to it actually happening. Self-talk is talking, more or less coaching yourself into believing good things are going to happen. In my wrestling career, it was convincing myself that I was going to win and it enabled me to fight through tough matches when adversity struck.

The physical training was also a big part of why the perfect storm hit. We trained hard. From two-hour practices to morning running, life as an Islander wrestler was intense. Every practice, as much as time allowed, covered all three positions. Some drilling, live wrestling, or breakdown teaching in neutral, top, and bottom. Sometimes it meant drilling on our feet, then teaching technique on

PURPLE REIGN

top, and going live in all three positions. Sometimes, it was a hard drilling practice with minimal live wrestling. I never wanted to overemphasize any one aspect of wrestling for long periods. Every position is important.

Technically, I wanted kids to be able to find some go-to takedowns and systematically have a baseline group of techniques. I would then allow them to branch out to some techniques that maybe fit their style or body type.

Some kids could be great upper-body wrestlers while others needed to have an arsenal of leg attacks. But all kids need to know how to set up their offense, and all wrestlers need to know how to defend leg attacks.

It starts with fundamentals. Once a strong foundation with fundamentals has been laid, a wrestler, regardless of age, can begin to expand their arsenal. I believe most techniques work – otherwise we couldn't use them to be successful. However, if a wrestler doesn't have the fundamental positioning down and some baseline technique, it won't matter what you teach the wrestler. The success level will most certainly have a ceiling short of true potential.

We spent a large portion of our technique work on basic fundamentals. It was a struggle at times, especially in those seasons after winning state titles, to really want to expand our arsenal. I realized early on that focusing on fundamentals would pay a much larger dividend. Therefore, in the spring when I was ready to expand our technique, I had to remind myself I was essentially starting over with a new group and had to return to the fundamentals to prepare them.

The relationships I built in wrestling is what it comes down to. I learned early on that I had to have the wrestlers' trust and faith to make this all work. Not every kid I coached did I just "click" with. Nor did they fall in love with me right from the beginning. Many would challenge me to the end of the time we shared as coach and athlete. I had to work hard to build a rapport with every kid. With some of my athletes it was easy. With others, I had to work at it. Personalities don't always mesh and people think, act and believe differently. That never hindered me from working at building a relationship.

If a person, kid, wrestler, whatever can believe in me as a leader, coach or person and know I care about them personally, I can get him to do more than they believe is possible. My greatest teachers, coaches and mentors did this for me and they inspired me to be more than I thought was possible.

Humans have a need for community or family. Every kid I coached needed something to be great. Some had it all and just needed a push. Some needed everything and I tried to provide as much as I could for them. Once the athletes believed in what they wanted to achieve, they grew immensely. Coaching became easier, wrestling became easier, leadership became easier and our relationship grew stronger.

I will always love those who I coached in one way or another. Some may not know it and others know it well. I want them all to know I poured myself into them and into this sport to lay the foundation in their lives for a greater purpose.

I love those young men that I worked with and built relationships with. I wanted them to excel and greatness was the expectation.

Wrestling was the vehicle. I can't think of a better sport, game or activity to participate in that parallels the ups and downs in life.

The young men that I coached will always hold a special place in my heart.

Having the opportunity to coach them and guide them was a dream come true for me.

It was a heck of a ride.

CHAPTER 12
DEDICATION

The man I believe to be the greatest Grand Island Islander wrestling fan and maybe one of the greatest Islanders of all time is Rod Shada.

Rod is a Grand Island Senior High Athletic and Nebraska Scholastic Wrestling Coaches Association Hall of Famer.

I met Rod in 2003, when I took the head wrestling coaching job in Grand Island. I knew his name because of his sons, Damon and Brandon, who were high school wrestlers around the time I was competing at the high school level.

I knew Damon from when he was coaching at Gordon High School in western Nebraska. I was recruiting that area while I was at Dakota Wesleyan University in the late 1990s. Brandon was certainly one of my contemporaries as we wrestled at the same time in high school

Upon my arrival in Grand Island, Rod made it a point to introduce himself to me, and we quickly became friends. It seems like it works that way when you are tied so closely with wrestling, you meet other wrestlers or wrestling people.

Rod was a counselor and past wrestling coach at Grand Island Senior High. He was a mix between a father figure, friend and a fellow wrestler. That binds us all by a mutual respect because we know the pain and agony we have been through.

In my first conversations with Rod, I realized he was an extraordinary person. Not because he had so many great achievements, but because he had the ability to make people feel great. His ability to hold a conversation and then end it leaving the other person not only feeling great about him/herself, but also by captivating the other person.

I never left a conversation with him unsatisfied with how I felt, but I always left unsatisfied because I wanted more. I wanted to talk more about everything from life to wrestling from birth to death and all points between. He could captivate an audience like few I had been around. And it seemed like there was always a crowd. He was like the famous person you always wanted to have alone to talk with.

He had an upbeat, positive attitude and was able to provide wisdom and advice. He genuinely cared deeply about the people around him. He also was a great listener who was always available to talk.

Later in our relationship, Rod's health declined after initially being diagnosed with cancer in 2012. He rebounded and seemed to have it beaten. Only to have it return and ultimately claim his life in June of 2017. I visited him in the hospital during his battle. He was in good spirits and I can only hope my visit brought him some joy. I know I took great joy in conversing with him as I had so many times before. Shortly after a visit in the hospital, I realized how special Rod was and posted about it on social media:

I visited Rod Shada in the hospital today. I'm not sure how to quantify my relationship with him, not that I feel I need to, but he isn't really a father-figure or a coach to me, I never wrestled for him. He was a mentor to me early in my time at GISH, as a coaching mentor. He is a friend, but we pretty much spend all of our time together talking about wrestling. I guess the best way to describe my relationship with Coach Rod Shada is that we are both crazy-wrestling coach/fan/enthusiasts.

As I thought about that driving down to Hastings College after our visit today, I found the real definition of my relationship with Coach Shada – he is one of the greatest "uplifters" I have ever been around. To define my term "uplifter" it is a person who after you interact with him/her you walk away feeling better about yourself.

HOW GRAND ISLAND BECAME A NEBRASKA WRESTLING DYNASTY

I have figured out that I have used Coach Shada as an "uplifter." I would expect that certainly doesn't make me special. He is the ultimate "uplifter" and he loves people. I suspect that while I feel special to him, and I believe I am, so is every individual that comes in contact with him. He is special to others by how he makes people feel. As I thought more about this, I felt like I used him and I felt selfish in my interactions with him over the years as I was "taking" from him. Then I realized he was taking from me too and he "takes" from every person he interacts with. He has built a rich life interacting with people and through his kind words and uplifting, he in turn feels good, too.

Then I thought that he is the ultimate giver and that makes him one of the richest people I have every met! That made me realize even more I have no need to quantify our relationship, nor do I need to make sense of this disease which has stricken him. I just choose to cherish our time together and strive to live my life in a way that I may too gain some of the true wealth of human existence, the gift of giving emotionally to everyone I come in contact with. Thank you, Coach Shada for setting the standard of "uplifter!" Not that I need to tell you this, but keep giving as I know you will and keep receiving, as I know you will too! I'm not special, but I love you for who you are and how you have made me feel in countless interactions! I only hope I was able to give a tiny joy back to you and made you feel good too. You deserve these riches!

God Bless you my friend!

After Rod's passing, I went to the funeral. By this time, I was working for the Truck Center Companies, which is owned by Trey Mytty. Trey is a cousin to Rod's children on their mother's side. I found out later that Trey's father, Guy Mytty, and Rod were good friends.

It was amazing to see the crowd. The company was well-represented, as Damon has a similar rapport with people as Rod had. It was at the funeral I realized how small I was in this world. At the same time, I realized the impact Rod had on so many people. I thought I was special and important. I found out he had that same relationship with hundreds, if not thousands, of people.

PURPLE REIGN

This book means a lot to me to have the opportunity to tell my story. It also is a labor of love. I share my love in this project for my former wrestlers and to some degree for all wrestlers. Anyone who has the courage to toe the line and get after it all by himself is who this book is for.

I am thankful to the people of Grand Island and the people who helped make the wrestling program great. They allowed our kids and myself to do our best to reach our potential. History was made, but the relationships are far stronger than the achievements. That is the true story and the love you find in these stories.

Rod Shada, in a lot of ways, is an inspiration to many. He certainly inspired my work in this book. I want to personally dedicate this book to him, in his memory. Rod was a true and great Islander, a lover, a fighter and a wrestler with a passion that overflowed and was shared with many.

I would like to thank others who have inspired me and many who are chronicled in this book.

Without these folks, I would be but a shell of the man I am today. To my mom and dad, you laid the foundation and fostered my love of sports. You gave me love, nurturing and every opportunity to chase my dreams. You sacrificed so much to teach me the right way to do things and the right way to live. You taught me about Christ and allowed me to grow in His love. You are my greatest example of love in this world. I love you!

My early wrestling coaches, Duane Dobson and Pat Cullen, you added to that foundation and built me into a young man. Rich Tomazewski and Dale Hall, you refined me and honed my skills and techniques for the battle of college wrestling and life on my own.

You passed me off to Rodger Jehlicka, who took a young man battle-tested and forged a warrior through the heat of fire. You shaped and polished my skills, and took me to the mountain top. I thank you for building me, not only as a wrestler, but as a human being. Each of your coaching examples taught me how to coach and how to love. I have drawn on those examples and experiences time and again.

HOW GRAND ISLAND BECAME A NEBRASKA WRESTLING DYNASTY

Scott Dobson, one of my friends in wrestling and from my childhood. Scott was one of my earliest of neighborhood friends. He was my example of a wrestling teammate, friend and champion. To my high school teammates and main training partners – some I beat regularly and some punished me – but I learned from them all. The 1980s Alliance wrestling teams were the warriors I looked up to. I knew if they could do it, I could do it!

My college teammates were the fire that pushed me and took me to places I never thought I could go. They were my best friends and the ones I know I could call on at any time – these guys I would go to war with! And in many ways, I already have. They strengthened me and I thank them. My brothers, I love you!

The countless wrestlers I coached, too many to name, but thank you for all you did. You made me proud and you built cathedrals through your blood, sweat and tears! I watched you grow into men. I pushed you and challenged you. I picked you up when you fell. I held you when you cried and celebrated some of your great moments. I thank you for sharing your lives with me.

I want to thank those people not mentioned. There are never enough pages, never enough thanks to dole out. Each of you, from the athletic offices, trainers, assistant coaches, strength coaches, parents, custodians, fellow teachers, administrators, bus drivers and so many more deserve my greatest gratitude.

Thank you for pouring into me and making me a better coach, person, parent, husband. This book is for you!

It wouldn't have been possible to complete this book without two driving forces who made this project become a reality.

I want to thank Trey Mytty. Trey is a powerful business man, but also a compassionate man. Trey is the owner of the Truck Center Companies, and he generously assisted with this project. Trey was a successful high school wrestler who learned from his father, Guy Mytty, a Hall of Fame high school coach in Nebraska. Trey's love and passion for wrestling and the lessons it teaches helped make this book possible, A huge thanks goes out to Trey!

Second, my co-author Craig Sesker helped me tell this story.

PURPLE REIGN

Craig is a very accomplished writer and he took this project on and told the story. Without Craig's help, this would be a jumbled mess in my mind and likely wouldn't have come out as eloquently. Thank you, Craig for your help, support and friendship.

My boys, Dylan, Caden and Keyan, my love for you is beyond what can be on paper in black in white. I only hope to give you what my parents gave me, everything they had. I'm talking about opportunity. I hope I have given you each the strength to endure, the fearlessness to fail, the tenacity to grow, the resources to chase your dreams and the ability to pour yourselves into others. You will never regret giving to others and strengthening them. I've learned the more you give of yourself the more you receive in return. Do this and you will have a full life.

Finally, to my wonderful wife, Kelli. You have endured much and fought through for a husband who was not always there. And even when I was there my mind was often on wrestling and other people's kids. Your loyalty is unparalleled, your love unwavering. You stuck through it all with little thanks and in so many ways you deserve much more. I thank you for always being by my side and giving so much of yourself to me and our boys. You have allowed me to do my thing even when it took time away from you.

When I've needed your support, you were there. Thank you, my love!

Mike Schadwinkel
November 2019

GRAND ISLAND HISTORY

STATE TOP THREE TEAM FINISHES
First: A/1973, A/2009, A/2010, A/2011, A/2012, A/2013
Second: A/1983, A/2015
Third: A/1991, A/2014

INDIVIDUAL STATE CHAMPIONS: 36
1959-Tom Terry, A112; Bud Ottman, A103
1963-Bob Sutter, A165
1967-Tom Meier, A145
1973-Gary Baldwin, A138
1974-Gary Baldwin, A138
1975-Fred Hotz, A126
1984-Joe Hostler, AHwt.
1988-Gary Pedersen, A189
1990-Brian Kelly, A145
1993-John Morrow, A119
2003-Efrain Ayala, A135
2005-Caleb Tyler, A275
2006-Brandon Hudiburgh, A189
2008-Isaiah Aguilar, A112
2009-Andrew Riedy, A103; Blake Fruchtl, A112;
    Alec Chanthapatheth 130; Nate Westerby, A215
2010-Andrew Riedy, A119; Blake Fruchtl, A125; Carlos Rodriguez
    Bueno, A130; Matt Rice, A135; Nate Westerby, A215
2011-Trey Trujillo, A112; Andrew Riedy, A130;
    Carlos Rodriguez Bueno, A140; Michael Bolan, A145

PURPLE REIGN

2012-Dante Rodriguez, A106; Andrew Riedy, A138

2013-Dante Rodriguez, A120; Trey Trujillo, A132; Chase Reis, A195

2015-Billy Thompson, A170; Edgar Silva, A195

2016-Gage Grinnell, A285

GI UNDER MIKE SCHADWINKEL

DUAL MEET RECORDS

2003-04: 9-4
2004-05: 11-2
2005-06: 4-10
2006-07: 9-5
2007-08: 14-5
2008-09: 20-1
2009-10: 17-3
2010-11: 16-5
2011-12: 19-1
2012-13: 20-2
2013-14: 17-3

Overall record 156-41

STATE MEDALISTS

2004

Brandon Hudiburgh 3rd at 160

Logan Hayman 4th at 130

Jake Reinert 5th at 145

Eric Wieland 5th at 215

2005
Kenny Guerra 6th at 103
Chad Davis 6th at 119
Logan Hayman 2nd at 135
Jarrett Carpenter 6th at 145
Brandon Hudiburgh 2nd at 171
Caleb Tyler 1st at 275

2006
Isaiah Aguilar 6th at 103
Brandon Hudiburgh 1st at 189

2007
Alex Sheldon 5th at 103
Alec Chanthapatheth 6th at 125
Riley Allen 5th at 130
Nate Roe 4th at 140
Jason Brisbin 6th at 160
Nate Westerby 5th at 189

2008
Isaiah Aguilar 1st at 112
Matt Rice 5th at 130
Tyler Glover 5th at 135
Riley Allen 4th at 140
Jason Brisbin 6th at 160
Alan Taylor 6th at 171
Nate Westerby 6th at 189
Jesse Janulewicz 2nd at 215

PURPLE REIGN

2009

Andrew Riedy 1st at 103
Blake Fruchtl 1st at 112
Carlos Rodriguez 2nd at 119
Mike Bolan 4th at 125
Alec Chanthapatheth 1st at 130
Matt Rice 3rd at 135
Riley Allen 2nd at 152
Beau Jepson 5th at 160
Coleman Westerby 6th at 171
Alan Taylor 2nd at 189
Nate Westerby 1st at 215
Cory Frankenberg 5th at 285

2010

Trey Trujillo 4th at 103
Andrew Riedy 1st at 119
Blake Fruchtl 1st at 125
Carlos Rodriguez 1st at 130
Matt Rice 1st at 135
Cameron Mettenbrink 3rd at 145
Beau Jepson 5th at 160
Coleman Westerby 6th at 171
Alan Taylor 2nd at 189
Nate Westerby 1st at 215
Cory Frankenberg 4th at 285

2011

Dante Rodriguez 2nd at 103
Trey Trujillo 1st at 112

Tanner McClaren 3rd at 119
Luke McGregor 5th at 125
Andrew Riedy 1st at 130
Carlos Rodriguez 1st at 140
Mike Bolan 1st at 145
Billy Leetch 3rd at 152
Jeff Brisbin 5th at 171
Coleman Westerby 2nd at 189
Daniel Sotelo 3rd at 285

2012
Dante Rodriguez 1st at 106
Matt Bolan 3rd at 120
Trey Trujillo 2nd at 126
Andrew Rojas 4th at 132
Andrew Riedy 1st at 138
Austin Leetch 4th at 145
Carlos Rodriguez 2nd at 152
Chase Reis 2nd at 170

2013
John Mottl 5th at 113
Dante Rodriguez 1st at 120
Matt Bolan 2nd at 126
Trey Trujillo 1st at 132
Haris Talundzic 5th at 182
Chase Reis 1st at 195
Edgar Silva 2nd at 220
Juan Medina 5th at 285

PURPLE REIGN

2014
Skylar Schmidt 5th at 113
Dante Todd 5th at 132
Andrew Rojas 2nd at 138
Rigo Barragan 6th at 145
Billy Thompson 3rd at 170
Edgar Silva 3rd at 195
Chase Reis 2nd at 220

STATE RECORDS

MOST POINTS IN STATE CHAMPIONSHIPS
All Class-256, Omaha Skutt Catholic, 2008
Class A-252.5, Grand Island, 2009
Class B-256, Omaha Skutt Catholic, 2008
Class C-195, Valentine, 2017
Class D-241.5, Amherst, 2014

MOST STATE PLACEWINNERS, ONE YEAR
All Class -12, Millard South, 2006
        12, Grand Island, 2009
        12, Amherst, 2014
Class A - 12, Millard South, 2006
        12, Grand Island, 2009
Class B - 11, Omaha Skutt Catholic, 2007, 2008
Class C - 9, Tekamah-Herman, 1989
        9, Rushville, 1991
        9, Valentine, 2017
Class D - 12, Amherst, 2014

MOST PINS IN STATE TOURNAMENT
All Class-26, Amherst, 2014
Class A-25, Grand Island, 2009
Class B-19, Omaha Skutt Catholic, 2008
Class C-17, Valentine, 2014, 2017
Class D-26, Amherst, 2014

MOST PINS IN DISTRICT TOURNAMENT
All Class-30, Tri County, 1999
30, Omaha Skutt Catholic, 2006
30, Central City, 2011
Class A-25, Grand Island, 2012
Class B-30, Omaha Skutt Catholic, 2006
30, Central City, 2011
Class C-30, Tri County, 1999
30, Valentine, 2017
Class D-28, Amherst, 2014